This is a work of fiction. All of the characters, organizations, and events portrayed in this novel are either products of the author's imagination or are used fictitiously.

www.melodramapublishing.com

Library of Congress Control Number: 2010926183
ISBN-13: 978-1620780282
Mass Market Edition: October 2013
10 9 8 7 6 5 4 3 2 1

Interior and Cover Design: Candace K. Cottrell
Cover Photo by Torrence Williams

Books by

NISA SANTIAGO

RETURN OF THE cartier Cartel

NISA SANTIAGO

Buy

for Melodrama

PROLOGUE

Expiration Date

"I'm not going to tell you one more muthafuckin' time, Jason. If this bitch doesn't tell us what the fuck we wanna hear, you better put a fuckin' slug in her head. Do I make myself clear?"

Jason exhaled, trying to regain control of the situation. He had no idea how he'd gotten put in this position. He tried desperately to block out Cartier's loud bickering, but her voice was like a sledgehammer drilling into his skull. In his opinion, Cartier had lost sight of the real enemy, in her thirst to avenge her best friend's murder.

Jason, holding the Glock tightly in his left hand, paced up and down the small motel room on the Conduit in East New York, Brooklyn. The motel was a run-down, rat-infested joint, where an addict would OD almost once a week, and where a steady stream of prostitutes brought their tricks. Management was on that "don't snitch" policy, which kept the steady flow of cash coming in.

"Look . . . ummm . . . what's your name again?" Jason asked, cautiously.

Through her whimpering, she managed to say, "J-J-Jalissa."

"Right, right. Jalissa, I don't want to hurt you, but I will make you swallow a muthafuckin' bullet if you don't tell me where the fuck Ryan lay his head at. I'm tired of running all around this city chasing a nigga with my dick in my hands. Now, with or without you, that nigga is ghost. The only question is, do you wanna take that ride to hell with him? You feel me?"

"But I told you I don't know where he lives," Jalissa whined, her voice trembling. "He's too smart to tell anyone."

Jason turned to Cartier. "I told you this is a waste of time! She don't know shit. If

you'd just let me control this shit my way, I wouldn't have to go through all this aggravation. I'ma flat-line that nigga in due time. Just let me deal with dude my way."

Cartier wasn't interested in Jason's sermon. She wanted results. She landed yet another punch in the side of the girl's head. "He's your fuckin' sister's man! Don't say that stupid shit again, or I promise I will kick your fuckin' teeth down your throat, you dumb-ass bitch!" Cartier spewed, jealous of the beauty sitting in front of her.

"Look, Cartier, I'ma handle this situation. Go home, and let me do what I do."

Cartier paused, her wild eyes darting back and forth from Jason to Jalissa. She was so angry, her throat tightened up.

Jason took her silence as an opportunity to exert more authority. "I do my dirt all by my lonely, and I don't need my wife, the mother of my seed, involved in this here gunplay. Now I'ma rock this bitch to sleep, but you gotta get ghost—"

"Now wait a fuckin' minute," Jalissa interjected, cutting Jason off mid-sentence. Out of fear, her eyes popped open wide like saucers. Her once flawless face was distorted with dried blood and bruises, compliments of Cartier. Her breathing was shallow as she struggled to maintain a steady stream of air to her lungs; she feared that one of her ribs might be fractured or broken. The last thing she thought could ever happen to her while getting ready to head out to the manicurist was that she'd be beaten, kidnapped, and then have her life threatened over a nigga she wasn't even fucking. This wasn't her beef.

"Shut the fuck up!" Cartier roared, her face twisted, enhancing her already strong features. Her anger was boiling over, and she knew she'd snap any second.

The prisoner wanted to plead her case and try to reason with Cartier, but at that point she realized she wasn't dealing with a rational person. She looked to Jason for reassurance, and he gave her a slight head nod that finally put her heart at peace. Up until then, she didn't know which way he'd flip.

Cartier took a couple steps behind Jason and seemed to relax. Finally she said, "OK, Jason. I'll let you take over, but I'm not leaving here until she tells us where Ryan lives. It seems as if this friendly line of questioning isn't working, so I think you should begin torturing this silly bitch. And I mean some real crazy shit, like cutting off a finger or something, because, as you can already see, this bitch can take a good beat-down and she won't break."

Cartier reached in her back pocket and pulled out a switchblade and tossed it to Jason. Her icy eyes caused Jalissa to shiver with fear.

Jason knew Cartier wasn't going to let Jalissa off the hook. Right now all he wanted was for Cartier to leave. And from the vicious ass-whipping Cartier put on Jalissa, he was sure all Jalissa wanted was for Cartier to leave as well. Jason exhaled a sigh of defeat, sweat trickling down his smooth skin.

Cartier's feminine voice turned gruff. "Cut . . . this . . . bitch . . . up!"

Jason ignored her order. Who the fuck did she think she was? Didn't she realize he was running the show?

As he struggled to think of another angle to try to outsmart Cartier, he heard, "Just as I thought—*Boc*! *Boc*! *Boc*! *Boc*!"

The sound of the loud cannon was deafening to Jason's ears. He watched in horror as Cartier let off four shots, each piercing its intended target. As he watched Jalissa's life and that of his unborn child drain from her eyes, it was only then he realized that Cartier had known about his affair all along.

Before Jason could retaliate or avenge the murder of his mistress and unborn child, Cartier emptied her clip into him, and the hot slugs ripped through his limbs. As his body hit the dirty rug, he heard Cartier say, "Now, fuck that bitch in hell!"

CHAPTER 1

Rewind

The Ivy, Chateau Marmont, Mr. Chow, TMZ paparazzi, and Sunset Boulevard weren't enough to keep Cartier in Los Angeles. Jason, on the other hand, was star-struck. The small, quaint Melrose Place-type of apartment that they'd rented on Larrabee Street—with the legendary Viper Room on the corner, where actor River Phoenix allegedly overdosed—cost a grip, though it wasn't any bigger than a Brooklyn bathroom.

The size of the apartment didn't really seem to bother Jason because he was hardly there. Every night he'd leave Cartier home alone with the kids while he'd hit every hot spot Cali had to offer. To escape the apartment, Cartier and the kids spent most of their time in the courtyard pool, where Cartier sat thinking about her life. Escaping New York was what she thought she'd wanted. A new beginning in a new town. Right now, Monya and Shanine were intuitively calling her to take action, and once again she knew she had to take her place as the head of Cartier's Cartel.

As Cartier sat by the pool watching Christian and Jason Jr. flop around in the water, she decided that as soon as Jason woke his tired ass up from a night of partying, she'd confront him and kick-start their return to New York. Looking at the celebrity-obsessed, fake-boobed wannabe actors coming in and out of the courtyard, she quickly grabbed the kids and toted them upstairs before she lost it.

Cartier put the kids down to take an afternoon nap. The apartment reeked of alcohol, which was obviously seeping out of Jason's pores, his loud snoring rattling her nerves.

Unbeknownst to Cartier, Jason had come home around seven o'clock in the morning after beginning his night by taking Mari, a new exotic beauty he'd met a few weeks ago, out to dinner at Eva Longoria's restaurant, Beso. Then he dropped her off and headed to club Villa, a swanky establishment littered with the rich and famous, before ending his night at celebrity hotspot, Ecco. Among the glitzy nightclub's regulars were Paris Hilton, Jamie Foxx, Gerard Butler, and one of the cast members from HBO's *Entourage*, to name a few. Jason had the pleasure of stalking them all.

The crumpled hundred-dollar bills tossed on the dresser along with Jason's brand-new platinum and diamond jewelry were an obvious indication of how much money he was blowing. In this town, you could only act your way or buy your way into the in-crowd. Jason was clearly doing the latter.

Cartier had estimated that in only three months he

had blown nearly a half million dollars as she sat back and said and did nothing, evidently still mourning the events regarding her friends. Now she was getting her mojo back, and wanted revenge so badly, she could visualize it.

Before waking up Jason, Cartier grabbed his jeans he'd taken off only hours earlier and his cell phone and crept back out of the room. She had never snooped on her husband—ever—thinking, if you search, then you shall find. And she really couldn't reason why she was doing it now. His jeans didn't hold any evidence of cheating. He only had his car keys, gum, and a pack of Gummy Bears.

Next, she went through his cell phone's rolodex. At first glance, everything seemed innocent. There were numerous male names, and all the females in his phone were either mutual friends, or family.

Cartier decided to go back and revisit the six unknown male names, two with Los Angeles area codes, and one of which he'd called right before coming home. She went to that number first and hit redial. Her heart raced as a female voice groggily picked up. Cartier hadn't given a thought about what she'd say, but she knew she wasn't going to just hang up.

"Hello," the female answered.

Silence.

"Hello?" she said again.

Thinking quickly, Cartier whined, "Oh my God, Jason's been arrested." Her voice was rushed and wavering. "He gave me his phone and asked me to call you. The police were everywhere this morning."

Cartier heard some rumbling, and could sense some hesitance.

"Who is this?"

"Oh, sorry. I apologize. I'm still shook up. My name is Sabrina. I work at the rental unit he lives in. I think they arrested him for a DUI. All I know is, one moment I'm on my way to work, and the next minute, he's tossing a phone in my face, asking me to call you and for you to bail him out. What's your name? He said to dial Marvin and ask to speak to his girl."

She giggled lightly. "That's my code name, Marvin, but my real name is Mari."

Her voice is syrupy-sweet, Cartier thought. *Seductive.* Cartier's jealousy was bursting, but she knew it was better to contain it for now.

"You two are crazy." Cartier forced a laugh. "Why do you have a code name? Are y'all like James Bond, 007 type thing going on? I know me and my man are into games, but that's usually saved for the bedroom."

"Oh, we have our bedroom games as well, but that's not what the code name is used for. Let's just say, my having a code name is what's needed to keep the peace." Again, she giggled.

"I see. Well, Mari, bail money—that's why I'm calling. Do you have any to contribute to getting Jason released?"

The giggling suddenly ceased.

"How much does he need? I have the five grand he just gave me to pay for maintenance for my condo this month, but I'm not really willing to part with that right now. And just between you and me, Sabrina, I'm not trying to dip into my savings, you know? Us girls gotta take care of ourselves first."

Cartier swallowed hard. "Well, he's been calling his cell phone constantly, and he said to tell you that whatever you give up, he'll double as soon as he's released. You seem like a smart girl. In less than twenty-four hours you could double your money."

"He said that?"

"Yes. But I'm only the messenger."

"No, no, I totally understand. But whatever Jason has promised this far, he's always come through, so I know his word is good. I just wish he would call me directly."

"In this day and age, who memorizes telephone numbers? I'm sure he would if he could, but right now, let's concentrate on getting him out. There's a couple of dollars in this for me as well for running all his errands. He needs twenty thousand dollars. Do you have that?"

Cartier wanted to know what this chick was working with. She was hoping for Mari to play Big Willie and toss twenty large in her hand, because she had every intention of not only kicking her ass but also keeping every dime.

"Yes, I have it, but I'm not giving up that much cash. I mean, I wouldn't feel comfortable. I can offer up the five grand, that's it. Besides, that won't be too much trouble, being that it's still sitting on my dresser. I haven't had a chance to do my banking yet. I've just booked travel to go on a holiday, so things are hectic."

Book travel? Holiday? This bitch think she is Posh Spice, Cartier thought. "But he said he'd give you back dou—"

"I know what he said, but I say no fucking way!" Suddenly the soft-spoken, eager-to-help woman was no more. "Either I give up the five, or I give nothing. He can take that and get the rest from his wife or some other chick, but that's as far as I go."

"Yes, yes, of course." Cartier didn't know how to play this out without Mari becoming suspicious, so she decided to give her a false sense of control. "I think I know where I can come up with the rest of the money, being that anyone's investment will be doubled. So do you want to meet me at the jailhouse? Shall I come and pick you up? Tell me, what should we do next?"

"*We* aren't going to do anything. Look, Sabrina, I don't mean to sound rude, but I'm not about to go on this odyssey with you. One girl to the next, I just walked through the door only hours ago. I need my sleep because I have an important evening planned ahead. Why don't you come over here, pick up the money, and go and spring Jason out of jail? And if you promise to tell him only good things about our talk, then there might be an extra hundred bucks in it for you from me. Are we cool? Are we on the same page, sweetheart?"

"Definitely."

Cunt.

CHAPTER 2

Tricks Are for Kids

Cartier couldn't drive fast enough to Mari's house. She had to see in person the female with the silky voice her husband was tricking with. Jason dropping that kind of money on a broad was definitely intimidating to her. You didn't drop that kind of money on a one-night stand. In fact, Mari was garnering more maintenance than Jason's own household. Jason was putting her before his wife and kids. While he had Cartier and his family living in a two-bedroom closet for three grand a month, his mistress was living in a high-end condo, and he was paying five grand for her pussy.

Mari's condo was located in Beverly Hills, where apartments ranged anywhere in a soft market from 1.5 to 8 million dollars. It took Cartier a matter of minutes to sum up the situation. Mari was either connected to the rich and famous, or she was rich and perhaps even semi-famous. She most likely met men to maintain her lifestyle, and Jason was exactly the type of asshole she preyed upon.

When Mari opened the door she was everything Cartier didn't want to see. Her beauty was unblemished.

Her creamy, mocha-colored skin, pointy nose, slanted eyes, and high cheekbones gave her an exotic look. She was a mixture of something you couldn't put your finger on. Her shiny hair was pulled back in a loose ponytail. Her long, flowing white silk bathrobe trimmed in white mink with matching stiletto slippers was something a character in a movie would wear. Cartier wondered, *Do women really dress like that for bed?*

Cartier was about to pounce on Mari and beat the beauty out of her as she opened the door, but the wide, warm smile radiating from Mari did something unexpected. Cartier's anger toward her rival subsided, as she stood in awe.

Extending her hand, Mari said, "You must be Sabrina. Welcome to my humble condo."

"You mean, *palace.*" Cartier's eyes scanned the immaculately decorated room. *Who is this woman?* Cartier thought. *And how did Jason land this one?* Mari looked to be at least forty years old. You couldn't actually see it from her face, but her age was in her eyes.

"Come sit down while I go and get the money."

Cartier got a firsthand view of Mari's baby grand piano, sheepskin fur rugs, Marilyn Monroe pictures, marble floors, granite countertops, and stainless steel appliances, and she wanted to be upgraded.

Jolting her out of her trance, Mari said, "So, how long have you and Jason been married?"

Cartier was stunned. *How did she know?*

"I didn't know until I opened the door. He showed me a

picture of you and the kids, cute kids by the way."

Cartier's anger immediately resurfaced. She was usually the one in control. For years she'd controlled The Cartel, and then her marriage to Jason. She was used to calling the shots, but here this Sherlock Holmes-type tramp was blowing her element of surprise. It was at that moment Cartier realized the hot California sun had fried her street sense. She was furious.

"Bitch, don't be questioning me! I should—"

The small chrome .22 was enough to silence the feisty Cartier. Her eyes flew open wide like saucers.

"Look, let's not go there, OK? The yelling and name-calling really isn't my cup of tea. It's beneath me. And it should be beneath you as well. You have kids? I mean, what were you planning on doing? Coming over here to fight me? And then what? You can't say that you'd actually feel better."

"Well, what would you do? I'm tired of cheap, low-life bitches like yourself fucking around with my husband, knowing that he's married. Don't stand here and act like you're so much above me, when all you are is a high-priced whore! That's right." Cartier's head bobbed up and down. "If you didn't have the gun, I'd beat you to a pulp, and I know I'd feel good about it. I'm almost tempted to still do that shit. Just because you got a gun don't mean you'd fucking use it!"

Cartier's body language tensed up. She was actually thinking about bum-rushing Mari, feeling dissed standing there with a gun pointed at her. How could she live that down? What if Mari told Jason that she'd pulled a gun on his wife and his wife didn't do shit?

"Two things are certain at this moment. One, if you even gesture impolitely, a bullet will rip into you without hesitation. And, two, please don't let my manicured fingertips fool you into thinking I can't handle a weapon. Yes, I did grow up with a platinum spoon in my mouth, but while vacationing in Bora Bora, or the equestrian training, we also shot quail in the summer months in the Hamptons. I've said all of this to say, never underestimate your enemy. I will shoot accurately, I will shoot to kill, and I will not feel any remorse, so it's in your best interest to not make me feel threatened. My trigger finger might jump."

Cartier realized she might be in over her head. Mari wasn't following the rules. In Brooklyn, if you had beef, you settled it, scrapping in the streets, and may the best bitch win. This lady was talking about plans, enemies, and quails, the kind of shit Cartier didn't care to hear.

"If you didn't have that gun, I'd wipe that cocky look off your face."

Mari giggled and tossed the envelope with the five grand toward Cartier. "What's the Brooklyn expression— If *if* was a *fifth*, we'd all be fucked up? Luckily for you, I've been dealing with all sorts of characters half my life. If you haven't already figured it out, I get paid for my services, and in my line of business, you have to always be prepared for whatever, whenever."

"You're a whore?" Cartier couldn't believe Jason had

resorted to paying for pussy. He was losing all his "cool" points.

"Jason doesn't think so. Besides, I like to call it a professional companion. Now take the five grand and forget my address because, I promise you, although you might think I'm easy prey for the angry wife, I'm not. I've dealt with an assortment of deranged, angry wives, and you are by far the least challenging. You're still young, dumb, and you have a lot to learn. And if you don't learn to grow up quickly, the love for your husband will put you in a precarious situation that you can't get out of. I learned a long time ago the art of war and how to plan out all angles of a situation, to avoid walking head-on into a trap. Instead of getting five grand tossed in your face, it could have very well been lye. Now, please get the fuck out!"

The last line did it. It was too much for Cartier's ego. No one spoke to her like that. No one!

Cartier lifted her left Nike Air and kicked Mari dead in her "professional" pussy. The sharp pain caused her to double over and drop her weapon to the floor. With all the strength she could muster, Cartier stomped the beauty out, until Mari stopped squirming around on the floor. At one point Cartier's foot came down so hard, you literally heard bones cracking.

Mari screamed out in an agonizing cry as a few of her ribs broke. She tried as best as she could to ball herself up into a fetal position, but that failed to protect her.

Without thinking, Cartier grabbed Mari's gun, aimed it point-blank at her head, and pulled the trigger.

Click. Cartier stepped back. *Click. Click. Click.* She tossed the gun to the ground and grabbed Mari by her long, silky hair and dragged her kicking and screaming into her bedroom. She needed the additional privacy to muffle Mari's screams.

"Oh, you thought shit was sweet." The first punch nearly broke Mari's jaw. "You wanna play gangsta bitch! Next time, load your fucking pistol. Now I'ma whip your ass, and you'll wish you had bullets in that burner!"

Cartier was beyond frustrated on so many levels. As much as she tried to leave the hood and hood life behind and live for her kids, she just kept getting dragged back into the game. Not only did Jason's actions keep bringing out her bad side, but she realized there wasn't any way she could be two separate people. She couldn't be Missus Homebody raising two kids, and also the head of The Cartel, with a beef to settle. The old Cartier would have never walked into that trap. She could have been killed, murdered by a mistress, all over Jason's dirty dick.

After leaving Mari beaten and bloodied, Cartier sat in traffic on Interstate 405. At that moment, she vowed to not only embrace who she was, but also to never, ever get caught slipping again.

CHAPTER 3

Queen B

Back at the apartment, Cartier couldn't believe Jason was still asleep. She'd left the kids with Elaine, an elderly woman who lived on the ground floor of the complex. She decided to confront Jason before picking up her babies. She really didn't know what would go down once she confronted Jason about Mari, and she saw no need to subject them to any hostility. What she did know was, she was mad as hell for being disrespected. Words couldn't describe how she felt about her husband's mistress pulling a gun on her. Sure, Cartier whipped her ass, but her pride was bruised, her ego was damaged, and her feelings were hurt. But what Cartier hated to admit was that Mari was right. She did run over there unprepared, without a clue as to who this woman was. She could have walked directly into a trap and be dead, just as Monya and Shanine had run into a trap.

Cartier looked at Jason with disgust. "Get up!" she roared, startling her sleeping husband.

"Damn, Cartier. What the fuck? Why you gotta be screamin' and shit like that? You know a nigga just came in."

"Get the fuck up because we need to talk," Cartier stated through gritted teeth.

Jason tossed his eyes in the air and shook his head. He was in no mood for Cartier's constant bickering. He thought he'd scream if he had to hear one more time about the hood's whodunit mystery. Yeah, when it all first went down, he was just as amped on finding out who shot the girls. But now, in Cali, he'd mellowed out.

Last night he'd kicked it with Jamie Foxx. For all Jason knew, he could get a bit part in a movie or something, so he decided to share this news with his wife. He sat up in bed, oblivious to his wife's anger. All he had on his mind was reliving last night.

"Yo, check it, ma. Last night I was at Ecco, and guess who the fuck I was kickin' it with all night? Guess." Not allowing Cartier to actually guess, Jason blurted out, "Jamie Foxx! Me and dude was poppin' bottles and makin' it rain all night up in the bitch. I mean, everybody was all on my dick!"

At that moment Cartier realized that Jason was too far gone for reasoning, arguing, or pleading. He was a full-fledged groupie, and she no longer wanted any part of him. She walked over to the closet and began tossing clothes into her suitcase, just enough to tide her over in New York until she went shopping.

"What are you doing?" Jason asked in a panic.

"Me and the kids are leaving. Tonight. We're moving back to New York."

"No, the fuck, you're not!"

"Watch me."

"You're not taking my kids back to all of that bullshit. I won't allow it."

"OK, no problem. Then they can both stay here with you and Mari. I'll come and visit them on the holidays. But I am going back to New York, and if you try to stop me, I'll fuck you up!"

Jason paused for a second, searching for the right words. He knew he was busted, but he didn't know whether this was about his cheating or if it was about Monya and Shanine.

"So that's what this is about? Some bitch I don't give a fuck about? You gonna let a bitch run you out of town? I thought—"

The slap was swift and accurate. As Jason tumbled backwards, Cartier spotted the empty Corona bottle he had left on the dresser from the previous evening and broke it on the wall. In a series of rapid events, Cartier had the jagged bottle tucked snugly at Jason's throat, his eyes exuding fear.

"If you ever go against me again for any reason, whether for a bitch or a nigga, I promise you that you *won't* live to regret it. Now, I said we're leaving. We got a muthafuckin' murder to solve. Now get your silly ass showered and dressed 'cause we're catching the red-eye out of this bitch. Tonight!"

CHAPTER 4

Hello Brooklyn

Cartier and Jason didn't want too many people to know they were back. As far as they were concerned, the fewer, the better, so the run-down, navy blue Ford Mustang was the perfect low-profile vehicle to come sliding back through Brooklyn on the low. They had one mission: Rock Ryan to sleep and then move on with their lives. They both assessed that it should take less than a couple weeks for Jason to get the drop on Ryan, and hopefully, although they knew things would never go back to normal, they would be able to put their lives back on track and move forward.

The two had only stayed in Los Angeles a few months after hearing the news from Bam about Ryan allegedly being the one to murder Shanine and put Monya in a permanent coma. Cartier wished Monya would wake up and tell them what actually happened on that fateful night.

Just as Cartier had asked, Trina had Bam, Li'l Momma, and Janet all waiting for their arrival. The familiar apartment felt like home to Cartier, her mind quickly recalling better years; a time when all the crew members were breathing.

Jason took Jason Jr. and Christian into Cartier's old bedroom to play with Prada and Fendi, while the adults all gathered in the living room to converse.

Cartier and Jason both looked worn and haggard from their journey, not to mention the stress and strain of recent events. Everyone was anxious to get to the bottom of what happened, and Bam, thus far, was the only one with the answers.

"So, Bam, tell us again. What's the word on the curb?" Jason sat down on the sofa, the plastic slip cover crackling under his body weight.

Bam began to shake her head wildly, and her eyes darted around the room. When she felt she had everyone's attention, she said, "It's like I was telling Cartier. Big Mike called me and said shit wasn't adding up, that the last time he spoke to Monya she said she was on her way to hit Ryan off, and then she'd keep going south to meet up with his boy, but as you know, she and Shanine never made it there."

Everyone sat in silence, dissecting the limited information.

Jason spoke up. "Yo, how we know Big Mike ain't tryna throw shit in the game and have Ryan take the fall on some Lee Harvey Oswald shit?"

"What?" Cartier looked at Jason sideways.

"Lee Harvey Oswald was the guy the CIA planted to take the fall for assassinating President Kennedy when we all know—"

Trina interjected, "Shut up, muthafucka, with your silly-ass conspiracy theory. This the fucking hood, and those muthafuckas ain't bright enough to hatch these elaborate CIA strategies. This was a straight jux, robbery, stickup! They saw their mark, and they took it."

"I agree with Trina," Janet said. "I don't think Big Mike would be clever enough to lure my baby down there, murder Shanine, and then pin it on Ryan. If he called and said the last person to see them alive was Ryan, then Ryan gotta get it."

"Well, if you ask me, I think we should hear Jason out. Y'all not giving Big Mike enough credit. Don't sleep on them 'cause they ain't graduate from high school and don't have any plans on going to college. These niggas all got their Ph.D's in hustling. Street smarts can take you a long way, and for all we know, Big Mike could be setting up Ryan to get got. How do we know they didn't leave Ryan and make it to Big Mike and his boys and they were set up?" Cartier's mind was racing. "At this point I don't know who to trust. I know Ryan, and he's just not built to rob anyone. That's just not the Harlem style. Harlem niggas are, and have always been, about *making* money, not *taking* money. Taking money is definitely a Brooklyn thing."

"What the fuck you tryna say?" Jason roared so loud, Jason Jr. burst into tears in the other room. "You sound like you still sweet on that nigga."

"I don't give a fuck 'bout no Ryan! And who the fuck you screamin' on?"

"You coulda fooled the shit outta me. Right now you sound like his cheerleader up in here cheering 'bout how he make money. Like he the only nigga that touch paper.

That nigga ain't have a dime for you when you got locked down."

Cartier hated to admit it, but Ryan doing her dirty when she got locked up for Donnie's murder still hurt, and she was in no mood for Jason to be exploiting her feelings in front of everyone.

"What that got to do with Monya and Shanine?"

"It got everything to do with them. You in here swinging from that nigga balls, and he could very well be the one who put their lights out."

"Now, y'all, calm down," Trina scolded. "Jason, all we're doing here is trying to get to the bottom of what happened. Let's not lose focus. This isn't about Cartier and Ryan. Nor is it about you and Cartier. This is about two young women both being shot in the head and left for dead, and until I take my last breath, I will keep trying to find out who took those girls' lives. They were both like my kids." Trina took a long drag from her Newport cigarette. "I practically raised all of them. They were over here so much with Cartier."

The whole room got silent, all of them reminiscing on the past.

Li'l Momma spoke up first. "OK, so what do we know? We know Shanine and Monya left New York heading south with weight, to make some paper. We know they were supposed to hit off Ryan, and then continue south to hit off Big Mike's little man. We know—but it's not confirmed—that they never made it to Big Mike. So as far as I'm concerned, we have our usual suspects, Ryan and Big Mike. Now all we gotta do is hit the streets and find out as much as we can about the last moments of Shanine's and Monya's life. And once we do that, we'll be led to their killer or killers. One thing is for sure," she added, "everything done in the dark will come to light. All we gotta do is wait."

"Wait? I don't have time to wait. My life is on hold until I find out who tried to put my son's mother's lights out." Jason was beginning to feel the weight of the situation. He realized that although his son was being raised by him and Cartier, not having his biological mother in his life would surely affect him.

"I'm with you, Jason," Janet said, her voice cracking. "As long as my baby lies in a coma fighting for her life, I can't function properly. I can't eat, I can't sleep. All I can think about is getting revenge. Whatever it takes, I want the person who did this to Monya dead."

"I feel you," Jason said. "And whoever it was, whether it was Big Mike or Ryan, once I get close enough to them, then it's a wrap. I will lullaby either one of them."

"Get close enough to them? So whatchu sayin'?" Janet asked, her tone taking a menacing turn.

"What do you mean, what I'm saying?"

Jason, like everyone else, was lost in confusion, not really knowing what Janet was trying to get at.

"Well, now you're talking about if you—"

"I never said *if*."

"OK, but you talking as if it's that difficult to murder someone. You a street nigga. What do you mean, once you get close enough to them? If you see either one of them in broad daylight, then guess what? Then you're close enough to them."

"Now hold on, Janet." Cartier realized that everyone, including her, had put avenging Shanine's murder and Monya's attempted murder on Jason's shoulders. She remembered the same pressure being put on her shoulders after Donnie had beat Bam just inches from being retarded. "Jason will handle the situation as he sees fit. He doesn't owe anybody anything, including Monya. You're asking him to go blazing niggas in broad daylight, trading in his life for Monya's. He has two children and a wife to think about."

Janet couldn't believe her ears. Especially from Cartier. Cartier's words to Janet were just as piercing as when the police had called to tell her that her daughter had been shot at point-blank range in the head and had little chance of surviving. Images of the rifts between Monya and Cartier throughout the years began to play in Janet's head and spill out of her mouth.

Janet's voice had elevated to a high-pitched shrill. She was beyond angry. Cartier represented everything her daughter no longer had—love, life, children, and a husband. Monya couldn't be any of those things because she lay half-dead in a non-descript hospital bed. Janet knew she and Monya would never lock eyes again. That she would never be able to see her smile, give her a hug, or cook a simple meal for her. Death was so final, and no one—other than Jesus Christ, her Savior—could come back from the dead.

"How dare you stand up in my face and talk about being a wife and a mother when my child no longer has those luxuries? And you called yourself her best friend. The head of the Cartel." Janet made a lemon-sucking face; she was that disgusted. "And her lover!"

Trina began sensing that things were going to get combative. "Janet, let's not go there. All Cartier is saying—"

"Ma, you don't have to speak for me. I'm a grown woman." Cartier stood and began to approach Janet, whose body had stiffened from stress.

Everyone immediately jumped to their feet to intervene the inevitable. As they began to hold back Cartier, Janet began flipping.

"Nah, don't hold her back," she taunted. "Let her go, so I can whip her ass, like I should have done years ago."

"You must got me mixed up with some lame-ass bitch because I will wear you out in here, Janet. I'm begging you not to push me."

"Don't let my age fool you, Cartier, because a bitch still got her hand game, and I will take out all my frustration on your ugly ass."

Hearing the word *ugly* was enough for Cartier. She charged at Janet, relentlessly, but Jason, Bam, Li'l Momma, and Trina created a barrier that neither Janet nor Cartier could break through. After a minute of struggling, Cartier and Janet both gave up.

Janet then collapsed onto the sofa and just cried her heart out. "They took my baby away from me." She sobbed.

"My only child is nothing more than an empty shell."

Everyone stood around, panting heavily from the commotion, their hearts hurting from the loss, especially Cartier, who sat down and embraced Janet, and they clung onto each other and cried for Monya.

As the evening began to wind down, after apologies were exchanged, everyone vowed to keep their ears to the streets to elicit any information that could lead to the person or persons who killed Shanine and tried to kill Monya. Everyone agreed that Ryan was the prime suspect, and that they needed to investigate Big Mike as well.

CHAPTER 5

Whodunit

What happened to Monya and Shanine was no longer the hottest news on the block. The hood had other crimes and murders to spark interest. But for Cartier and her family, Monya and Shanine were their number one priority.

For the moment, Cartier and Jason didn't have a choice but to temporarily move in with Trina. They moved into her old room, Trina moved to the pull-out sofa, and all the kids—Prada, Fendi, Christian, and Jason Jr. all moved into Trina's room with the understanding that all of this would be temporary. Everyone was on edge in the small, cramped apartment.

Jason was hardly around because he was back to hustling to support his family, leaving Cartier and Trina in the confines of the run-down apartment. When Jason came strolling in at three o'clock in the morning, Cartier was up, waiting.

She told him, "I'm not comfortable with you out in the streets all day and all night, leaving me and Christian in here all day. I told you back in Cali those days were done. And you better not be out there with no bitch 'cause I will fuck you up first and then beat a bitch down. You hear me? I'm tired of playing the dumb-ass wife role."

"Come on, ma. I'm not in the mood for this shit right now," Jason said, dismissing her with a wave of the hand.

The gesture annoyed Cartier. "Oh, you think I'm joking?" Cartier yelled and woke up Trina, who was asleep in the living room.

"All right now, y'all. I ain't in the mood for no drama. Those kids gotta get up for school tomorrow."

"Sorry, ma'am." Jason then turned to Cartier. "Shhhhhh. Ain't nobody in the mood for your late-night bullshit."

In a hushed voice, she replied, "I'm not happy, and shit has got to change."

Jason certainly didn't want to fight, and he also knew the quickest way to end an argument was to fold. It was late, and they both were exhausted.

"A'ight, let's discuss this in the morning. Tonight, I just wanna fuck my wife . . . eat your coochie until you come in my mouth," he said in a low-tone, slapping Cartier on her ass. "That is, if you want that too."

A large grin spread across Cartier's face. She wanted to remain angry, but the love for her husband superseded, as she followed him into their room.

&⊸◉

Christian was always an early riser, so either Cartier or Trina tried to be up before her because, within seconds, she could get into a heap of trouble, from messing with the stove and allowing gas to seep out if the pilot light wasn't lit to actually searching for matches to set something on fire.

This morning Cartier beat her daughter up, and as she went into the kitchen to fix breakfast, the unmistakable squeal instantly turned her stomach. She'd been hearing the familiar squeal all her life.

"Christian, come in here and look at the mouse," Cartier called to her precocious child.

Christian came flying into the kitchen and stood silent. The fat mouse was squirming around, trying to get its body off the sticky glue mouse trap perched on the kitchen counter near the Sara Lee bread. You could see the bread crumbs mixed with mouse droppings where he'd eaten through the plastic.

"Don't touch it, OK."

"I don't wanna touch it. I wanna rub it."

Cartier laughed. "You can't rub it. That's nasty."

"Why?"

"Because it's not a pet. It's a rodent."

"But why?"

"*But* your butt into the bathroom and go and wash your face and brush your teeth."

Christian didn't move. To say she was hardheaded would be an understatement. She looked around the kitchen as she calculated her next move.

Meanwhile, Cartier was already tossing the bread into the trash can along with the squealing mouse, knowing this wasn't the first or last mouse they'd catch. "Why are you still standing here?"

Christian's eyes went toward the top of the refrigerator. "My stomach is rumbling for that white cake."

Cartier looked at the vanilla cake Trina had baked over the weekend. "Go and take your ass in the bathroom and get ready for school!"

The loud outburst from Christian's wails had woken up all the kids. She'd screamed as if she was getting her ass torn to pieces, though Cartier hadn't even touched her. Cartier knew she and Jason were raising a cry baby, using a different approach to parenting, talking things out with the kids and not hitting as a form of discipline.

Trina wasn't as patient. "Shut up!" she roared, startling the four-year-old. "I'm telling you, Christian, you are begging for an ass-whipping, hollering like you stupid, so damn early in the morning. Now take your tail in that bathroom and get ready for school, and if I have to tell you twice, I'ma get the belt."

Reluctantly, Christian marched off, to Cartier's relief. She had told Trina on numerous occasions to not hit her daughter, but Cartier knew her mother was only two seconds from putting the smack down.

After the children were off to school, Cartier wanted to resume what she'd started the night before. She fixed Jason breakfast and called him in. Once seated, he began to tear into his plate of food, never lifting his head up, although he knew Cartier wanted to talk.

"What are we doing here?"

Jason held some of the scrambled eggs on the fork and stared at his wife. He had no idea where she was going with the conversation. "What do you mean?"

"I asked, what are we doing here? Why are we here?"

"Like, why are we living with your moms?"

"You know what? Yes. Answer that question. Why are we living with Trina?"

"We're here because we got shit to do, and once it's done, then we're out."

"That's my point, Jason. We're only here because we got shit to do, but each day we're here, it's not getting done. We're squeezed in here like sardines in a can, and I feel like you're losing sight of what brought us back to Brooklyn. Why are we not getting any closer to Ryan? You got my mother sleeping on the sofa, all the kids piled up on top of each other. I can't live like this anymore. It's been two months to do something that I thought would take a week."

Jason dropped his fork and pushed his plate away. He lost his appetite. He didn't want to hear about murking Ryan. Truthfully, Jason had once again lost his passion to avenge anyone's murder. He was back in the streets getting money, and that was where his heart was. But he couldn't tell that to Cartier, nor was he saying that he wouldn't get at them niggas, but it just wasn't a priority.

"Cartier, why are you putting all this pressure on me? Don't you think I wanna handle my business? I'm out here getting money to take care of my family. I'm out on these streets day and night with my ears peeled to the curb, trying to get the right information to get at these niggas. I know I don't discuss it with you, but believe me, I got this."

"I just think you need to let me in on your plans. I'm not some green chick who grew up sheltered. I get down for mine, and I think I could help bring this situation to a head."

"OK, ma, let's talk. I'm all ears. Tell me what I gotta do, and it's done. Tell me how you want shit to go down, and I'll make it happen."

Jason could see Cartier's mood shift. He held up his index finger. "Hold that thought for one second." He ran into their bedroom and returned with a crumpled paper bag he'd brought home last night, pulled out the kitchen chair, and began to count out the stacks of money he'd just picked up. *Why not kill two birds with one stone?* he thought.

Instinctively, Cartier sat down beside him and helped him count it out, not bothered that he'd interrupted what was supposed to be an important conversation.

After a solid thirty minutes of business at hand, Jason said, "How much you got there?"

"Thirty-five large," Cartier replied. "How much you got?"

"Seventy."

"Is the count correct?"

"Hell, yeah. Those niggas know not to fuck with my bread. Now, what's on your mind? Let's square all of this away for good."

The pangs of jealousy hadn't actually subsided from Cartier's run-in with Jason's L.A. mistress, and when Jason spent long hours away from home, those negative feelings resurfaced.

"Things are going well with your business, and now you gotta take care of your family. I don't want to live like this, shacked up with Trina in this roach motel. I deserve better than that."

"I hear you, ma. And that's what I was gonna do anyway, but I got so much shit on my mind right now. I'm out here in these streets for us, not me. You think I'm out here up in the clubs partying, but most of the time, I'm in there making connections. In the clubs is where you see niggas who need product. A lot of deals go on in the sanctity of a nightclub."

Cartier looked at Jason like he had two heads. "Don't tell me that dumb shit like my name is Moron. It's insulting. You ain't up in the clubs solely for business. You're up in the club for the bitches!"

"See, I can't tell you shit, so I'ma prove it to you." Jason began to grab up the stacks of money. "I put a bounty on Big Mike and Ryan's head, and my man came through for me."

"Big Mike? Why him? And what type of bounty?"

Jason didn't have any bounty on anyone. He wondered if he should feel guilty about the small lie he was telling to keep peace in his household.

"Hell, yeah, Big Mike. He gotta get it too, and that's final. No more speculating on whether or not he was down. I've been thinking about this shit real hard. Last week after Janet came back from taking Jason Jr. to see Monya, she and I began to kick it, and we decided that we won't ever know for sure who pulled the trigger, so they both gotta get it."

Cartier took in his words. "OK, I feel you, but from here on out, you and I will decide things together. We're a team. Don't ever forget that. I should have been a part of officially adding Big Mike to the list."

Jason nodded.

"So tell me about this bounty."

"I put the word out to a few select, thorough niggas that I trust that I needed to get close enough to touch those lame-ass dudes. Anyone who could get me information, I got fifty large."

"Just for information?"

"True that."

"That seems like an awful lot of money. Don't forget you got a family to feed."

"Damn, Cartier, can't shit ever make you happy nowadays? All you do is complain. I thought I was doing exactly what you wanted. You been riding my back since we were in Cali. You just said shit is taking too long."

Cartier realized she did sound like a whiny, ungrateful child. "Babe, you're right. I'm sorry." She leaned in and gave him a quick kiss on the lips. "I'm just concerned, that's all. And I just want this shit to be over. I want both of those bastards dead, and I'll happily do the whop"—Cartier began doing the old-school dance—"over their graves."

Jason couldn't help but laugh at his wife's antics, but then he got serious again. "Well, that's why I need information on where these niggas rest at. Ever since they got word that I was back on the scene, those niggas don't even party no more. I heard Big Mike went back underground like a li'l bitch living with some trick in South Carolina. And Ryan, that nigga name should be Casper 'cause he stay ghost. I can't get no info on that muthafucka. No bitch name, no address. I can't even get what type of ride he driving. That's a clever dude. I heard he switch his shit up constantly from his cellie, to his whip, to his chick. He don't got no loyalty for nothing, but the bread."

"Fuck Ryan. He ain't God. He can get got just like anybody else, and he definitely ain't smarter than me or you. You giving him too much credit. Those moves he's doing is Hustling 101, and I'm not impressed." Cartier sucked her teeth and threw in an eye-roll.

"You better not be impressed, if you know what's good for you," Jason teased, looking at Cartier sideways.

Cartier exhaled and tried to gather her thoughts. She needed to focus and get a clear vision of what their future was going to look like. She didn't want to mention anything to Jason, but she kept getting a strange feeling that shit was going to go wrong. She was never one to worry in the past, but her gut kept giving off warning signs. She felt strongly that if they didn't find and kill not only Ryan but now Big Mike as well, then their lives were in imminent danger. If either one of those guys felt threatened enough to stay on the low, then Cartier and Jason needed to move in silence and lullaby them both before it was too late.

"Jay, there's so much I worry about, mainly our kids. You've had a long run out here in these streets, and we both know that that fast money don't last forever. I want our family to be straight. You can't keep spending money like it's water. We gotta keep stashing for that rainy day. If anything happens to either one of us, we both need to rest assured that Christian and Jason Jr. are going to be straight."

"Now why you gotta go and jinx a nigga?"

"I ain't jinxing you. This is what smart people do. They plan shit out to the very last detail, and that's how we gonna stay a step ahead of the game. Take the bounty off their heads and keep that money in our stash. I'ma get back out there and keep my ears open. You know chicks can't keep any secrets. Before we know it, we'll find out where Big Mike and Ryan are creeping."

"So that's how we should do it?"

"Most definitely."

"A'ight, but just watch who you asking about Big Mike and Ryan. Those niggas ain't stupid. If they hear from the wrong person that we been asking about them, shit could get ugly. And I want you to start carrying that chrome .25 I have stashed up in the closet. Wherever you go, you need to be strapped."

❧

Cartier missed connecting with Monya more than she could ever express. Admittedly, she didn't think about her each day because the pain was so powerful, but whenever she allowed her mind to travel back to the past, a steady stream of tears would inch out, and before she knew it, she was a hot mess.

All she thought about was, *What if?* What if they had been born into a better environment? What if their mothers had chosen better baby daddies? What if they weren't forced to hug the block because they were virtually starving from lack of food money? What if whoever decided to rob Monya and Shanine didn't feel as if they had to kill them?

The short ride to the hospital was consistent for Cartier twice a month. She'd bring a portable radio with numerous CDs of their favorite music, perfume, a comb and brush to style her hair, fingernail polish and remover to paint her nails and feet, and loads of gossip. Today she brought a mixed tape with a new female rapper named Nicki Minaj from Jamaica, Queens.

"What you think about this chick?" Cartier asked Monya as she began to remove the old nail polish to apply a new coat. "I'm trying to figure out what's all the hoopla over her. If you ask me, she's a Lil' Kim knockoff, minus the hard lyrics."

Cartier looked at the neon pink OPI color she'd just applied and loved it. "Listen to how she manipulates her voice. That's all Kim," she exclaimed, getting hyped for no reason. "Damn, Kim fell off. How you gonna let someone come and steal your style? A style that B.I.G. created and Kim pulled off. If you ask me, after B.I.G. got murdered and Kim dropped *La Bella Mafia*, she didn't put the sexy swag in her voice. She was just rapping regular, almost trying to sound hard like Foxy, but not realizing why we liked her from jump." Cartier held up Monya's hand to her face. "How that look? I'm hooking your ass up."

Cartier then got up and walked to sit on the other side of the small hospital bed, so she could paint Monya's other hand.

"Yeah, back to this Minaj chick. I'm not trying to make it a Queens versus Brooklyn thing, but you know those bitches always wanted to be us. And when I say *us*, you know I mean Brooklyn. Queens girls are some lame, wannabe bitches, and I'm fucking pissed that Kim ain't riding for us no more. She's moved from Brooklyn and went all Hollywood . . . talking about Hollyhood." Cartier rolled her eyes. "I should slap her face!"

Cartier knew if Monya was awake she'd agree with every word she was saying. "Anyway, Monya, as soon as you wake the fuck up and stop trying to hog all the attention"—Cartier laughed and playfully tapped Monya on her shoulder—"we could get back out there and do us and have these bitches worshipping us. We could even do something legal. You know"—Cartier looked off into space—"I was thinking we could get paid just for being who we are. This whole reality TV seems to be here to stay, and if we could get us a show, I think we could really blow up, you know, get our fifteen minutes of fame. And we wouldn't have to sell out either, like these fake-ass people manufacturing drama. Shit, we bring real drama every day, the real drama that people wanna see. And here's my thoughts. The show would be called *Cartier's Cartel.*" Cartier paused. "Oh, I know you just didn't flinch, bitch. I see you're still a hater. OK, how 'bout *The Cartel?* How that sound?"

Cartier looked at Monya and actually waited for a response. Then she continued, "Yeah, the camera would follow us as we roll through Brooklyn with real fights, checking bitches and niggas, and hugging the block. Imagine the camera rolling, back in the day when we fucked up Shorty Dip with our moms! The ratings would have hit the roof. Or how 'bout the time when we got busted for Donnie's murder? I can still remember the look on Trina's face when the police came kicking in the door."

Cartier laughed so hard, she almost couldn't stop.

"Wait. Imagine the camera catching the day you came to visit me in jail to tell me that you and Jason were fucking around and you were pregnant. I know the look on my face had to be priceless." She doubled over in laughter. "Wasn't that some shit? I know I must have looked like Boo Boo the Fool."

After about five minutes of silence with Cartier just staring at her friend with anticipation and a longing in her eyes, she got serious. "Monya, I know you're going to wake up soon. I know that in my heart, but I think Janet is losing her faith. You gotta do something to help her, Monya . . . open your eyes, squeeze her hand, do something 'cause she's starting to talk like you're already gone, and if something doesn't happen to change her outlook, then I'm afraid that she's gonna take matters into her own hands and try to kill Ryan herself. You know she has it in her, Monya—as do I, but I would prefer if she just let me and Jason handle this. I don't know what I'd do if something happened to Janet, or my moms, 'cause we both know where there's one there's the other."

Cartier fidgeted in her chair and then continued. "And I really hate to keep asking Janet to be patient, but that's what she has to do for right now." Cartier shook her head. "And forget about me and Jason keeping on the low. It took all of seventy-two hours for the whole world to know we were back but fuck it . . . what can you do?"

A few hours later Cartier was packed and ready to go. She leaned in and kissed Monya's forehead. "As soon as you walk out of here, I'ma whip your ass for all the stress you've put me through. But I'll let you get your weight up first. Love you, bitch."

CHAPTER 6

Brush Your Shoulders Off

Cartier awoke to an empty living room. The Christmas toys that were under the tree last night were no more. Her heart plummeted as her mind tried to focus on the obvious. Not wanting to wake up the kids only to have them distraught, she went and shook Jason awake.

"Jay, get up. I can't find the kids' toys."

Jason turned over with a huge grin on his face, and immediately Cartier was relieved. She didn't know what her husband had done with the toys, but by his reaction, she knew it was all good.

"Are the kids up yet?"

"No. I didn't wake them, but you know when they come out to see what Santa brought them and don't see shit, they're gonna flip."

"Go get everyone up and get dressed and—"

"What's going on?"

"Don't ask me any questions. Just do it. I promise you it's all good." Jason gave Cartier a soft kiss on the lips. "And Merry Christmas, wifey."

"Merry Christmas, hubby."

The five-bedroom, three-thousand-square foot beachfront house on Long Beach, Long Island nearly stopped Cartier's heart. The whole ride to their final destination, the kids couldn't stop asking where they were going, and where was Santa?

"Jason, what are we doing here?" Trina asked, perplexed.

Jason shut off his ignition, pausing for theatrics. "We're home."

Cartier's grin stretched as long as a football field. Was Jason telling the truth? Were they really going to live in this exclusive community? Had they really moved from the hood into this mini-mansion?

"Ma, what's wrong? Why you just sitting there?" Jason asked, suddenly second-guessing his decision to get the house and surprise his family.

"Wrong? No, baby, it's all right. I cannot believe you did this for us. I'm sitting here stuck on stupid but in a good way. Now this is how I want to be treated."

"Well, I know when you say 'we're home,' you mean, me too, right?" Trina already envisioned herself living in the lap of luxury.

"Yeah, Trina, there's enough room in here for all of us. We got five bedrooms up in this mutha!"

After everyone got out of the car, Jason escorted them into the house. The first thing the kids saw was their presents under the Christmas tree. In the middle of the night, Jason had carefully moved all the toys from Brooklyn into their new house. As the kids went crazy ripping into their presents, Jason showed Trina her new bedroom on the main floor.

Trina couldn't believe the opulence. She actually had a bathroom in her bedroom along with a walk-in closet.

"Trina, this is called an on-suite, where you have a bathroom and walk-in closet in your bedroom. This the new shit that's out now." Jason couldn't wipe the cocky smile off his face if he was paid to. He felt like a real man taking care of his family in the right way.

Trina, being a bit overdramatic for Cartier's taste, dropped down to her knees, tears streaking down her face, and kissed the imported Carrara marble floor. "I didn't think I'd ever live in anything like this in my lifetime. Jason, you're the best son-in-law I could ask for, and if Cartier gives you any trouble, just call me and I'll straighten her right out."

Embarrassed by her mother's antics, Cartier quickly snapped her mother out of her foolish behavior.

"Ma, stop actin' like you ain't used to shit!"

"Look, I don't got to put on airs for no muthafuckin' body. I'm keepin' it real. I ain't used to shit like this here, and neither are you. So kiss my ass!" Trina grinned.

As Trina got settled, Jason took Cartier upstairs to their master bedroom suite, which had all the amenities as Trina's but much more. There was a granite wet bar and French doors that led to a deck overlooking the Atlantic Ocean. The butter-colored sand below blew Cartier's mind. She'd never heard of Long Beach, though it was located right under her nose.

"How did you find this place?"

"This realtor put me on. Yo, I've been thinking a lot about what you had to say, and as a man, and your husband, I'll be the first to admit, you were right. I was thinking, if I'ma get at these niggas, I can't have my family at the front line. That was my first thought. My second thought was about that Mari shit."

Cartier rolled her eyes, her stomach churning. She didn't want to think about her. Especially at Christmas. But if there was one thing she knew about her husband, he would always try to right the wrong. And she was sure this was his apology.

Jason continued, "You had every right to leave me, but you didn't. And I know I keep fucking up. But what I'm trying to say is, here I was, like a stupid muthafucka, paying five large for this bitch rent, dropping a few pennies on a couple shopping sprees, when I got you and my kids living in a dump—"

"I hate when you try to come clean and confess to shit that's late. Nigga, I know you was tricking on that bitch. What makes you think I wanna hear about it now, on Christmas? You think I want that bitch to steal my joy?"

"See, you not getting me. That's my point. I'm trying to tell you I see the error of my ways, and that you and the kids, and Trina, y'all my family, and from here on out y'all come first."

Cartier wanted to argue some more, but what was the point? What do you say to your husband who speaks so casually about cheating, and then has the nerve to say in your face not only did he cheat, but that he'd dropped coin on his mistress? She decided to live in the now and enjoy the beautiful home she and her family deserved.

"So you're finally ready to get at those niggas?"

"I been ready." Jason scratched the side of his unshaven beard. "Now that we got this hideaway, my mind will be at ease about the kids. But I still want Trina to keep her crib as a decoy. I want the hood to think we're still there."

"That's a good look," Cartier said. "But for now let's not talk about murders and mistresses and just enjoy Christmas."

"Of course, we gonna enjoy our Christmas, but we got to agree on one thing. And drink it in before you comment. As I just said, I'm maturing and so should you."

"What is it?"

"No one, I mean no one, can know where we live. Not your little girlfriends, and none of my peeps. The only person who gets a pass is Janet. She literally our blood. But other than that, we can't put our lives or our kids' lives in jeopardy. And I know you trust your girls with your life, but females talk too much, and they might say something around the wrong person. So, please, obey me on this rule."

Cartier thought about his request. "Well, what will I tell them?"

"Tell them the truth . . . that your husband said they're not welcome."

"I won't say that, but I will tell them something."

A few minutes later everyone got a present they weren't expecting.

"Merry Christmas," Cartier sang into the telephone.

"Get to the hospital now. She's awake . . ."

You could hear the excitement through the telephone when Janet called.

"Ma!" Cartier screamed. "Monya's awake. We gotta go!"

The whole family piled up into Jason's Benz and rushed to the hospital. Janet, Li'l Momma, and Bam were already there. Cartier's face was flushed with happy tears because she knew in her heart that Monya was coming back. She was a fighter!

As Cartier rushed to her bedside, disappointment quickly sank in as Cartier looked down only to see that Monya wasn't awake.

"What happened?" Cartier asked, searching for answers in Janet's eyes.

"Cartier, she woke up for me. My baby spoke." Janet tried to choke back tears but was unsuccessful. A mother's love came pouring out. "She tried to speak, but all she could say was 'Momma . . .'"

"She really spoke?"

"Yes, she did . . . she wanted her momma."

"But," Cartier looked down at Monya. "Is she just asleep?"

Janet shook her head as the tears came flowing back down. "She slipped back in a coma—"

Li'l Momma interjected. "But she'll wake back up again. The doctors said that things like this can happen."

"Of course she will," Trina chimed in. "We all know

she's a fighter and she has too much to live for. And she's already proved that she misses us by giving us this Christmas present. Janet, don't give up. Monya will be back with us soon enough."

Everyone stayed at Monya's bedside, kissing her face, rubbing her head, and updating her on their Christmas. Jason went out and brought back takeout from the diner and they all made an evening thanking God for the miracle.

CHAPTER 7

The Cartel

Mink weather rolled around again, and Cartier, Bam, and Li'l Momma didn't disappoint. All three women were bundled up snugly in their luxurious garments as they hopped inside the deluxe CLS63 AMG Mercedes with the sleepy eyes. Cartier thought the windows were so small, it looked like a person with their eyelids hung low. The cookies-and-cream-colored car was Jason's latest toy, but for the moment Cartier and her crew were riding on 22's on their way to the Dominican beauty parlor, Sophie's, for a quick wash and set. Jason's vanity plates, H8TER, spoke volumes.

Tonight anyone in New York City who was well known would be going to Club Roxy for a New Year's Eve party given by Don Poo, a local promoter who always threw the best parties.

Cartier pulled up in front of the salon, so all the nosy bitches could see her ride. Then she told Bam and Li'l Momma that she'd go and park. It was no longer a secret that she and Jason were back, so Cartier felt that if people were going to run their mouths, she'd give them something to say, like how she pulled up in the latest whip.

Moments later she joined her friends. As Cartier came strutting through the doors, all eyes were fixated on her. She noticed a few familiar faces and exchanged head nods.

To her amazement, she saw a face from the past. Jynx from East New York, Brooklyn was in there getting her hair done. She no longer sported the crazy blond Mohawk style; it appeared as if she'd let her hair grow out and had darkened it slightly. The last Cartier had heard, Jynx had gone to live down South after all the drama that went down. Her best friend Breezy had tried to kill her by stabbing her repeatedly, trying to collect on some insurance scam. After that no one heard from her.

Cartier wondered what made her come back. She wanted to walk over and get the gossip, but Jynx was giving off the *I-don't-want-to-be-bothered* energy, so Cartier just kept it moving.

"What's up, *Cartier*?"

Cartier spun around to see a girl that reminded her of herself. The eldest of three girls, she was making quite a name for herself throughout the boroughs. She was the head of her own crew and hustling to keep money in her pockets.

"Whaddup, Apple? How you be?"

"I be good." Apple stood up, so Cartier could admire her latest gear. "Just tryna maintain."

"Maintain? You're all of seventeen years old. You better maintain your grades," Cartier joked. "How are your sisters?"

"It's all good."

"And your twin?"

"She still tryna be me," Apple joked about her twin sister, Kola.

"A'ight, take care of yourself and tell your fam I said whaddup."

"No doubt."

Bam was already at the bowl, and Li'l Momma was waiting around like everyone else. The salon was packed, and unless you did like Bam and chose an inexperienced beautician to do your hair, the wait was going to be long. Cartier told the owner, Sophie, that she'd wait for her to do her hair, and then she and Li'l Momma went and sat in the back.

"What are you wearing tonight?" Li'l Momma asked.

"My outfit is crazy. Jason bought me a red sheared mink coat for Christmas. That red mink with this skin-tight black and white Chanel dress is gonna fuck everyone's head up when I walk through."

Li'l Momma's face lit up. She knew Cartier had a shape most women would kill over. And she knew her mocha-colored skin would glow underneath a red mink coat. Before Li'l Momma could reply, she noticed a Spanish chick with a small mole over the top of her lip, and wild, curly, dyed blond hair staring at them. Dressed in the latest gear, she had on all the obligatory name brands—Prada boots, Gucci bag, and Seven jeans. *Cute*, Li'l Momma thought. But what wasn't cute was, why the fuck the bitch kept staring?

"Can I help you?"

The Spanish girl looked puzzled. "Huh?"

"You keep looking over here, and I was wondering why, if you needed something from over here."

The Spanish girl smiled graciously. "Oh, no, mommie. You look familiar. No worries. I'm sorry."

Li'l Momma relaxed. "No problem. My bad."

Cartier and Li'l Momma took one last look at the female and then resumed their conversation.

"So what are you wearing?"

Li'l Momma wasn't exactly sure. She knew tonight she could pick up a sponsor—a man who could sponsor her lifestyle—so her looking her best was imperative.

"I got two outfits, and I can't decide which one is best. I'm going to bring them both over tonight, so meet me at Trina's so I can try them on, and you can help me decide."

Cartier smiled. "Just like old times, huh?"

Li'l Momma was confused. It almost felt awkward for her. Usually it was Cartier and Monya who did these things together, like helping one another choose an outfit. She wanted to say something, but she didn't need to.

Cartier knew why Li'l Momma's mood had shifted. Both women sat in silence for a moment.

Cartier changed the subject. "Damn, Bam, you're almost done, and we didn't even get started."

The hairdresser had led Bam to the seat to begin roller-setting her hair.

"Y'all chicks are playing. It's too damn crowded in here, and I got so much to do to get ready for tonight. I'm going to take a cab back home."

"Nah, don't leave us. Stay. We got hours before the party tonight. You know we ain't rolling up in there until right before midnight. It's eleven o'clock in the morning." Lately all Cartier did was play wifey, so being out with her friends and having girl talk was really important.

Bam hesitated for a moment, searching for a way to duck out on Cartier and Li'l Momma. "I want to get my nails done and—"

"We gotta get our nails done too, so you might as well wait for us."

Bam didn't reply.

An hour later, Bam was gone, which annoyed Cartier. "Damn! Why Bam acting like that? I mean, we all came together, so we should leave together, right?"

Had Li'l Momma not been bored, perhaps Bam's secret would have remained just that a little longer. "I know why she left."

"Huh?"

"I said, I know why Bam left."

"Am I supposed to get three guesses?" Cartier asked. "Or are you going to just tell me?"

Li'l Momma looked around before whispering, "You gotta promise not to flip."

"Flip? Why would I flip? Just tell me the dirt. You know I don't like secrets."

Li'l Momma thought about that statement. Now she was annoyed. "Who does like secrets? What sense does that make?"

"Yo, Li'l Momma, I don't got time for this. You began this conversation," Cartier said, her voice slightly elevated. "Just fucking finish it."

"I am trying to finish it, but you saying stupid shit like, you don't like secrets. All I'm saying is, who the fuck does? And now you screamin' on me."

Cartier remembered she always had to handle Li'l Momma differently. She wasn't as easily intimidated as the others, nor did she ever allow Cartier to just scream on her. Cartier exhaled. "Just tell me why Bam left. Please."

Li'l Momma liked to demand respect from Cartier. Li'l Momma felt that, even as they grew older, Cartier still held on to the notion that she was their leader and that what she said was law. Although it was like that growing up, they were in their twenties now, so there was no way she was taking any flak from Cartier, who Li'l Momma thought was a bully. They should have all bonded together back in the day and put a stop to Cartier's bullying, but they didn't. In their own way, Monya and Li'l Momma always challenged Cartier, but not hard enough to get her to change her ways. Cartier was the spitting image of Trina, and Li'l Momma felt like, forty years from now, Cartier would still be just as immature as Trina.

Li'l Momma inched closer and lowered her voice. "Bam has been seeing Big Mike." She waited for a reaction. "Did you hear me?"

Cartier heard precisely, but shock had temporarily paralyzed her. Could this really be true? Could Bam really go against the grain?

"And how do you feel about that?" Cartier didn't know why those were the first words she chose; she didn't give a fuck how Li'l Momma felt.

"I think it's cool, but what I feel isn't cool is her keeping it a secret from you. She should have told you from jump."

Again, Cartier couldn't believe what this moron was saying. She knew she couldn't exactly explode in the crowded salon, but she wasn't going to condone the betrayal.

"Li'l Momma." Cartier leaned in and lowered her voice. "Bam fucking around with Big Mike is anything but cool. And that's not just my opinion. I would bet money that if we took a vote, it would be three against two. Me, Shanine, and Monya would all agree that you two have lost y'all minds."

Li'l Momma rolled her almond-shaped eyes. "You're not going to lay any guilt trip on me. First off, I'm not the one fucking Big Mike, and two, you can't speak for Shanine or Monya."

Cartier lost her cool and elevated her voice as she rose to her feet, and Li'l Momma followed suit.

"Oh, yes I can! If I don't, who will? Are you forgetting that our best friend is dead and Monya ain't in the position to give interviews? And for all we know, Big Mike had something to do with it."

"I ain't gonna ever forget what happened to Shanine or Monya, but I've kicked it with Big Mike, and he ain't the one. He's a good dude, and he's feeling Bam. So if Bam is happy, then I'm happy for her. Just because Shanine is gone and Monya ain't awake to enjoy her life doesn't mean that Bam has to stop her lif—"

The swift hook to Li'l Momma's right jaw loosened a tooth. The two-piece combination, both landing accurately, instantly dazed Li'l Momma as she visually lost focus. The barrage of punches were coming so quickly, she never had a chance to defend herself.

In all their years of friendship, Li'l Momma had always harbored a slight resentment toward Cartier. Thoughts of fighting with her had always circulated in her head, but somehow, getting beat down wasn't ever what she had envisioned. She thought she could have whipped Cartier's ass, but now she was getting dragged across the floor of the salon and getting pummeled by her friend. It felt like hours before a few people got up enough courage to break up the one-sided fight.

Li'l Momma gathered her things. "This shit ain't over, bitch! I'ma fuck you up!"

"You and what army?"

Cartier wasn't trying to hear Li'l Momma's beef. She had bigger fish to fry. She tossed two crisp hundred-dollar bills to Sophie for disrespecting her place and then sat down to finish what she'd started. She had a party to attend.

CHAPTER 8

What About Your Friends?

Cartier raced home after getting her hair set. She knew Jason would be home, since she had his ride. Of course, he was still sleeping, though it was slightly after three o'clock in the afternoon.

Still amped up after the morning's events, Cartier went straight in to speak with Trina. "Ma, where are the kids?"

"I asked Janet to take them for a while to give me a break. She drove over here this morning shortly after you left. All that hollering was getting on my last nerve. And if Fendi asks me one more time, could she put on her bathing suit and go swim in that cold ocean, I'ma jump out that damn window."

Both women laughed heartily. Cartier realized that lately Trina had been on edge. Living under Cartier and Jason's roof, Trina wasn't able to have company anymore, so Cartier knew her mother was tense. As much as she loved luxuriating in their new house, the downside was, it took away her freedom as an adult. Trina still felt like she had it going on and wasn't ready to be the old lady of the house.

"Well, I'm glad they're gone because I need to kick it with you."

Anticipating drama, Trina immediately perked up. Anything to put a spark in her dull life. "What's up?"

"I had to whip Li'l Momma's ass today."

"What? Why y'all fighting?" Trina lit up her Newport cigarette.

"Her mouth too damn smart. You should have heard some of the things she was saying."

"Who was saying?" Jason asked.

Cartier and Trina were so involved in the gossip, they hadn't heard him come downstairs.

"I'm glad you're awake. You need to hear this too. I tried to almost kill Li'l Momma this morning in Sophie's. Her raggedy ass should be happy she's still alive. I just started beasting on her."

"Get the fuck outta here." Jason's interest was piqued. "Give me the play-by-play."

"Yo, her mouth is too reckless. But y'all not gonna believe what I'm about to say." Cartier paused for effect. "Bam is fucking Big Mike."

There was a pregnant pause as both parties drank in the information.

"Is that bitch stupid?" Trina spoke up first. "If Janet find out, she will do Bam dirty. If Bam thought Donnie beat her brains in, Janet will choke the life outta her."

"Out of all people, I'm most shocked by Bam," Jason said. "All I wanna know is, how the fuck they got together? Word on the street was, Big Mike was in S.C., and all along he right in our backyard. You think she was gonna set us up?"

"At this point I don't know shit," Cartier responded vacantly. "All I know is, Li'l Momma think that shit is OK, and for that she got her ass beat!"

"I should go over there and whip her ass too, just on G.P.," Trina said, forgetting she was in her forties.

Jason didn't like what he was hearing. "You know you can't fuck with her no more. I don't want to hear y'all cool again and see her in my ride."

Cartier shook her head. "I'm not going to do her like that. The first thing we need to do is speak with Bam and hear her out. I need her to explain how she could fuck around with the enemy. But, in all fairness, we never did officially place Big Mike on the do-not-fuck list. The only people who said he had to get it was you and me, Jay."

"But she knew he was on our list of suspects." Trina wasn't about to let Bam get off easily.

"But we can all admit that Ryan was always the prime suspect, so let's cut her some slack, at least until I speak with her."

"So whatchu gonna do about Li'l Momma?"

"Fuck Li'l Momma. I need a subscription for all the issues she got. That bitch probably in ICU right now. She had the balls to basically write off Monya and Shanine, so she's lucky all she got was a beat-down."

Cartier sat down and began pulling off her boots. Today wasn't a good day for her. She hated to admit it, but she understood what Li'l Momma was trying to say.

She just didn't respect the way it was said. Li'l Momma was trying to show she was a good friend to Bam, now that one Cartel member was gone and to put it mildly one Cartel member was put on a permanent vacation. Cartier wanted the best for her friend, but it didn't have to be at the expense of justice for Monya and Shanine.

With a boatload of niggas out there to fuck, Cartier thought Bam just had to get over it. She crossed a line that should have never been crossed. They were a crew, and no nigga or bitch came before your crew. Bam would just have to choose which side of the line drawn in the sand she wanted to stand on.

"Do you think she called and told Bam?"

"I'm sure she did, but Bam hasn't called me yet. And that's fine, because I want to see her face-to-face."

"So check it," Jason began. "Before the sun comes up tomorrow morning, Bam is going to help us set up Big Mike. If she doesn't, then she's added to the list."

"What?"

Cartier's voice elevated to an unrecognizable shrill. She'd been through a lot, not only today but in the past year. The Cartel was dismantling. She didn't like that they used to be closer than sisters but were now seemingly archenemies. Cartier continually felt herself being pulled in so many different directions. Her loyalty was split in so many directions—her husband, her kids, Janet, Trina, her siblings, Monya, and Shanine. And she was constantly feeling like she had to carry all burdens. If it meant scrapping in the streets, then so be it. But the last thing she ever wanted to do was fight with Li'l Momma or Bam. Yeah, she was hyped after they fought. But now, with Jason talking reckless as if Bam wasn't like a sister to her, she had to question her own actions. If she wasn't respecting them, how could she expect her husband to? Especially when most men always wanted to shelter their chick away from their girlfriends.

"Who stepped to the side and crowned you boss?"

"Cartier, don't get cute in front of your mother 'cause I will slap the shit outta you in front of your mother. I ain't Li'l Momma!"

"Try it!" Cartier barked back.

"Ain't nobody slapping nobody." The last thing Trina needed was for Jason to get up enough gumption to try and hit her baby because, if he did, it would certainly be the last hit he'd ever attempt.

"No, he actin' like Bam is some stranger on the street. This is my sister he's talking about. I didn't even get to hear her side—"

"There ain't no side! And what about Monya and Shanine? Huh?"

"Jay, I gotta kick it with her first and hear her out. If I know one thing it's that Bam loved us all equally, and she wouldn't fuck with this kid if she felt like he had anything to do with what happened to Monya and Shanine. I just think it was a bad judgment call on her part."

"You sound crazy! You think that slow-ass Bam is smart enough to know if this nigga had something to do with what went down. Do you think that niggas really be admitting who they murdered during pillow talk? 'Cause if you do, I'm telling you right now, that's bullshit. Of course, he gonna tell her he ain't have nothing to do with what happened. He probably already swore on his momma's life and all that." Jason shook his head. "I just never figured you to be this gullible, Cartier. You're slipping." Jason walked out of the room, leaving Cartier with some scathing parting words.

Was she slipping? Visions of her time in Los Angeles, allowing Jason to run through her while she said and did nothing resurfaced. The cold, steel gun being pointed in her face as his mistress continually mocked her turned her stomach sour. In a matter of months she'd been called dumb, gullible, immature—a host of descriptions that didn't sit too well with her. Cartier needed time to reflect on her actions. Being dumb, gullible, and immature in the game she was in could cost her her life.

CHAPTER 9

Poppin' Bottles

It was a given that Li'l Momma would be unable to go to the party. What wasn't expected was, Bam tried to make an excuse not to go.

"What do you mean, you don't want to go now?" Cartier asked, grilling Bam.

"Cartier, I'm exhausted. I've been running around since this morning, and I just want to get some rest."

"Did you speak to Li'l Momma today after you left us?"

"Li'l Momma?"

"That's what I said. Did you not hear me?" Cartier replied sarcastically.

"Yeah, I heard you. But, no, I haven't spoken to her at all. Last I heard from her, you two were together," Bam lied.

"Well, unfortunately for you, Li'l Momma and I got into it today, so she won't be going to the party. And I didn't leave my husband and kids in bed today to get all glammed up to not go out and have a good time. So pretend this is tag, 'cause you're it. Whatever you have to do to get up enough energy, please do it and meet me at

Trina's house around ten. And, Bam?"

"Yes."

"We need to talk when you get there."

❧

A nervous Bam arrived at Trina's house looking her best. She felt that if she avoided Cartier then she would look like she had something to hide, when she felt secure about her relationship with Big Mike. She knew Cartier, hell-bent on seeking revenge for Monya, just wouldn't understand. She never asked Cartier what they needed to talk about because she knew.

Of course, Li'l Momma had called and told her that she and Cartier had fought over the fact that Bam was seeing Big Mike. When Bam took a taxi to Brookdale Hospital and saw the damage Cartier did to Li'l Momma, her own life flashed before her eyes. The last thing she wanted was to get on Cartier's bad side. She also felt sorry for Li'l Momma basically getting beat-down over her affair. Bam wondered how she'd gotten into that situation where she had to lie or be deceptive to her friend. She didn't plan on hooking up with Big Mike; it just happened.

Cartier knew Bam was on edge. Her facial expression was that of someone who'd seen a ghost. Cartier never brought the subject up. *Let Bam stew in her own guilt,* she thought. For the moment, all she wanted to do was party.

Cartier and Bam rode to the city in Jason's car. Jason and Wonderful would ride together, and he promised to meet her there.

The atmosphere inside the club was euphoric. All you saw were bright smiles and sparkling diamonds. Just as Cartier thought, all eyes were on her. A lot of chicks hadn't seen her out partying in almost two years. Now she was back and flyer than ever.

As Cartier and Bam mingled in the crowd, the party didn't really start popping for her until Jason and his Brooklyn crew came walking through. Bam noticed Jason and Wonderful first.

"Jason's here," Bam said, making a gesture toward the other side of the room.

Cartier scanned the room until she spotted him. She saw him trying to make his way over to the bar area but constantly kept getting stopped by men and women, most everyone recognizable.

Cartier recognized the Spanish girl from the salon. She sidled up close to Jason and watched his arm drop near the girl's waistline. His mouth moved rapidly as his eyes darted back and forth. When Jason spotted Cartier, a large smile formed. He tossed one arm in the air and kept moving toward her.

Cartier's eyes were like a hawk's. The Spanish girl never acknowledged that Jason walked away, and Cartier realized she was about to overreact.

Jason greeted Cartier with a kiss and immediately turned toward the bartender. "Give me three magnum bottles of Ace of Spades," Jason stated with authority. He turned back toward his wife. "Ma, you wearing the shit outta that dress."

Cartier smiled like she was Cinderella. "Thanks, babe."

"What's up, Bam?"

"I'm good."

"You looking good, too."

"You know it."

As the champagne flowed, the New Year countdown came and went, and as the music played, Jason and Cartier were oblivious to the elephant in the room. Perhaps an hour had passed before Cartier looked up and locked eyes with Ryan, who was surrounded by several Harlem niggas and a few chicks. She noticed the same Spanish chick a few feet to his right, laughing with another woman who favored her.

Reluctantly, Cartier gave Ryan a head nod, and he reciprocated. After taking another sip of her champagne, she wrapped her arms around Jason and pulled him in close. She began to gesture a slow dance.

"Don't look, but Ryan is here. Are you strapped?"

Jason pulled her tighter. "No doubt."

For the rest of the night, Jason, Wonderful, and Cartier only pretended to keep drinking. Actually all three of them sobered up quickly, wanting to be alert, to make it out of the club safely. Cartier thought if nothing jumped off, then that meant Ryan had no clue they suspected him of setting up Monya and Shanine.

As the night died down, Jason and Cartier both noticed that two of the young dudes rolling with Ryan were no longer around. So Jason had Wonderful send his little man, Blake, to the car to grab the other burner, and Cartier sent Bam to get the car. When Jason's phone began vibrating, he knew that was a cue from Blake to leave Ryan and his goons in the club.

As they approached the door, Jason gave his burner to Cartier and told her to walk directly to the car. He added, "Whatever pops off, don't look back. Just bounce. I'll be good."

Blake passed the second burner to Jason, and all three began to walk out the club. Cartier could see the white Mercedes from the distance. All they needed to do was walk a short distance in the brisk, cold air, and this night would be over. Just as Cartier was beginning to think that they'd overreacted, they felt Ryan and his crew behind them.

Jason looked over his shoulder and saw Ryan make a gesture. Thinking quickly, he reached for his burner. With his free hand, he shoved Cartier out the way and said, "Ma, bounce!"

Then it suddenly happened.

Boc! Boc! Boc! Boc! Boc!

Gunfire spewed, and everyone ducked for cover.

Cartier spun around and pulled out her burner and began blazing.

Boc! Boc! Boc! Boc! Boc!

Jason, Wonderful, Blake, and Cartier were surrounded. Ryan and his crew were shooting for keeps, and Ryan's young soldiers were racing down the block, their guns aimed steady on them.

Cartier was handling her gun better than she thought she could in five-inch heels and a dress. All she thought about was getting herself and Jason home safely to their kids.

As bullets whizzed by, pandemonium broke out. People started stampeding on each other, men were running out of their gator shoes, and women were dropping their designer bags to the ground in their quest to make it home to celebrate the New Year with their families.

Ping went the sound of the bullets as they bounced off the metal light poles, just inches from the domes of innocent bystanders.

They all managed to hop inside Jason's Benz, and with Bam at the wheel, she was able to maneuver and get everyone out of danger.

It took a few minutes for each person to come down from the adrenaline pumping through their veins.

Finally Jason broke the silence. "Yo, that nigga is dead. I swear on my fucking kids, his days are numbered. He gonna try to assassinate me with my wife?"

Cartier knew that now wasn't the time to be a girl, but the lump in her throat almost forced her to cry. She remained quiet until she could get a handle on her emotions. Finally, she got up enough gumption to speak.

"Somebody running their mouth." Cartier didn't have any qualms about cutting her eyes at Bam.

Fear made Cartier think irrationally. To her, Ryan hadn't surfaced in months, yet tonight he and his goons seemed too prepared.

Bam piped up instantly. "Well, it ain't me. I collect information, I don't give it."

"Well, if not you, then who? Ryan ain't built like that. He and his goons came there to assassinate all our asses. First off, how the fuck did he know we were gonna be there? And, second, how the fuck he know that we think he had something to do with Shanine and Monya?"

Bam's pressure instantly rose. "Cartier, you think you got everything all figured out, so you tell me how the fuck he knew. All you keep talking about is, you know Ryan, like you some psychic. Did you know his ass was gonna leave you when you did your bid? So please stop talking about you know how Ryan's built and what he would or won't do. For all we know, this could all have been a coincidence. It is New Year's Eve. Even murderers like to celebrate."

"You know what?" Jason began. "Bam, right now, I'm feeling you. You got a muthafuckin' point. I keep telling Cartier that dude ain't how she got him pegged. That nigga ain't no white knight. He grimy just like the rest of us Brooklyn dudes. I don't give a fuck what borough he rep. If you ask me, he didn't give a fuck about Cartier, and he damn sure didn't give a fuck about The Cartel. He deaded both your friends and straight took their keys on some gangsta shit. And if he had his way, he would have sent your dumb ass to the clouds and left your daughter motherless."

Cartier wanted to lean over from the backseat and punch Bam in her blockhead. And while she was at it, spitting in Jason's face would've surely curbed her anger. How did she become the bad guy? Ryan and his hit squad had just tried to murder them, so why were they screaming on her?

Before she could dig into them, Wonderful spoke up.

"I ain't really tryin' to hear all of that right now. Niggas just tried to dead me. We need to stay focused. Jay, man, you gotta handle your business."

"Oh, no doubt." Jason was too busy thinking about how to get at those niggas. And quickly. For a man who had put off this beef, he was suddenly sucked in. If he wanted to keep his life, he had to get at Ryan.

Cartier noticed that Jason was in deep thought. The whole car ride back to Brooklyn was quiet.

After Bam dropped off Wonderful and Blake, she headed toward their block to drop herself off.

"Yo, Bam, make sure you circle the block a few times, to make sure niggas ain't laying low on us."

Bam nodded in agreement.

After they thought it was safe for Bam to retreat to her apartment, Jason spoke up. "Bam, Big Mike gotta get it," he said. "Not now, but right now."

Bam's mouth fell open in shock.

"He gotta go, Bam. At this point, we don't know who to trust. Honestly, Bam, if you got a problem with this, then you gotta go too." Jason had his Glock pointed directly at Bam's side.

When she looked down, tears began to slide down her face. "Jay, how you gonna do me like this? I thought we were fam. I would never go against you or The Cartel. Don't you know we're like sisters?"

It was at that point that Cartier peeped that Jason had his gun steadied on Bam. Instantly, she was furious. Then, she tried to understand why he was treating Bam that way, and she understood. Each one of them could have had a tag on their toe at the morgue, had those bullets hit their intended targets. Cartier thought about Christian and Jason Jr. and understood perfectly. Bam would get over her feeling hurt about Jason pulling a gun on her. But if any one of them had been murdered tonight, how would their kids or family members have ever gotten over that? Bam fucked up by getting involved with Big Mike before the beef was settled. That was the bottom line.

"Bam, as Jason said, he gotta go. All that 'we're sisters' bullshit ain't music to anybody's ears right now, not when we just got chased out of a club with niggas gunning for us. So, as your sister, I'm waiting for you to give up the locale on Big Mike."

"Don't y'all think if I thought Big Mike had anything to do with Shanine and Monya, I'd kill him myself? You know I'm thorough, Cartier. I get down for my crew, but I've looked in his eyes. I've shared my bed with that nigga, and he ain't do it. He don't get down like that."

Cartier erupted. "How the fuck you vouching for this dude when you just barked on me for doing that with Ryan? As Jay said, he gotta go. And if you plead his case one more muthafuckin' time, then you gotta go too."

Bam felt trapped. She had no idea what they wanted her to do, but she was certain that if she refused, Jason would make good on his threat. And although she knew Cartier loved her, the fact that Cartier and Monya were the closest, and that Monya was in a coma, Cartier wasn't going to let anyone live who had a hand in that.

Bam wanted to tell them she didn't mean to fall in love with Big Mike; it just happened. It all started with him calling to give what information he knew about Shanine and Monya, and from there it blossomed into a real relationship. Big Mike promised to move Bam with him to his huge house in South Carolina. They even discussed having kids. Bam wanted to let them know Big Mike was a gentle giant. She knew in her heart that he would never have done to their friends what he was now being accused of.

Bam looked into Jason's and Cartier's wild eyes and knew they were meant to be with each other. They maneuvered and thought alike.

"What do I gotta do?" Bam asked hesitantly.

"You know where that nigga live. That's valuable information. Spill it, so me and Wonderful can go and handle my business."

Cartier said, "I'm not feeling that."

Frustrated, Jason exhaled. "What? What, Cartier? You're not feeling what?"

"I'm not fuckin' feeling you taking Wonderful. If there's one thing I know, it's the strongest muthafucka will crack under pressure, and I'm not losing you to no snitch."

"Snitch? My man ain't no snitch."

"Not today he ain't, but let him have five homicide detectives breathing down his throat, telling him they don't really want him, they only want you, and you tell me how the story will play out."

"OK, Bam, just give me the address. I'll do this solo."

"Would you just shut the fuck up for one second and check the plan?" Cartier rubbed her sleepy eyes. "Ain't nobody getting any sleep tonight. Bam will call Big Mike and tell him she's coming over for that after-the-club fuck—y'all know how that go—and when he opens the door, Jason, do you. Do it fast and quick. I don't want him to suffer. And I'll be the getaway driver."

"Cartier, no!" Bam cried. "I can't. And you want me to be there? I just can't. Why can't Jason take Wonderful? You're being cruel. You know I got love for him."

Cartier didn't have any sympathy for Bam. Deep down inside, she knew she had to do something, and no matter how much everyone tried to tell her that what happened to Shanine and Monya wasn't her fault, she didn't feel the same. She'd started The Cartel and introduced the boosting and drug-dealing to them. She was always the enforcer. The one who protected everyone. Had she still been at the helm of The Cartel, she was almost sure she wouldn't have walked into the same trap her friends had walked into. And since there was no changing the past, she could write the future with her own actions.

Al Capone had said, "You take one of my men and I'll take five of yours!" That's the same gangsta shit Cartier was on at the moment. Bam needed to suck up her tears. Everything Cartier did had a reason behind it.

"Bam, I wish shit didn't have to go down like this, but you did this to yourself. It's your bed, so you'll have to lie in it. As we said earlier, somebody running their fuckin' mouth, and if the heat get on us, all of us will have a life sentence hanging over our heads. And Jason knows he can trust me not to crack, and I know I can trust him. With you taking part in this, we can rest peacefully that you'll have something to lose as well. It gotta be like this, baby girl, so get over it and get to dialing."

❧

"What time is it?" a groggy Big Mike asked.

"It's a little after five in the morning, and I wanted to give you your after-Christmas present."

"Bam Bam, I'm tired, ma. Can't this wait until tomorrow? I got a special day planned for you."

A lump formed in Bam's throat. Choking back tears, she said, "I hope you don't got a bitch there."

Big Mike chuckled. He loved his feisty Bam Bam, as he called her.

Twenty minutes after Mike told Bam she could come over, he heard the faint knock at the door. Eagerly he envisioned opening the door to see Bam wearing a long, sweeping mink coat with nothing but naughty lingerie on. Instead, he got the remix.

"You already know what it is, nigga. Don't say a word!" Jason's eyes were menacing, his voice hoarse.

Big Mike's eyes darted toward Bam. He didn't know if Jason had followed her there and had ambushed them both.

"Bam Bam, you ain't down with this, right? This ain't you, right?"

"Nigga, shut the fuck up!"

The butt of Jason's gun pounded on the back of Big Mike's head. He took the pain like a man and allowed himself to be duct-taped to a chair, arms and hands. Had he known there wasn't a cavalry waiting outside for Jason, that the real intention wasn't to rob him but to kill him, Big Mike would have fought for his life.

"Jay, you ain't got to do me like this, man. Not over no paper. Whatever you need, I got you, kid. I'm not a tough guy. I'm just a businessman."

Hmm, Jason thought. *Why not? Ain't this what Cartier said Brooklyn niggas do?* "Where ya stash at?"

Big Mike was disgusted. If he made it out of there alive, he would personally put a bullet in Bam's head. What else could he do? Forgive her? His heart was broken.

"Bam Bam knows where the stash at. Ain't that right, Bam?" Big Mike stated.

Jason couldn't believe his ears. Big Mike was one stupid muthafucka. You don't let no chick, unless she wifey, know where you keep your stash. *He must really be feeling Bam.*

"Is that so?" Jason said with a slight twang to his tone that annoyed Bam. She knew he was being facetious at her expense. "Well, Bam Bam"—Jason broke out into laughter—"could you do the honors?"

Reluctantly, Bam walked over to a huge chest and pushed it back from the wall, exposing a handmade hideaway. As she dropped to her knees to retrieve the money, Big Mike couldn't help but taunt her.

"Damn, Bam Bam, you set a nigga up over some paper? I thought I gave you all you needed. I guess you wanted it all," Big Mike said dryly. "And to think I was gonna wife you for real. Not no hood-title shit either, but the real deal. Make that shit official. But I guess a thug bitch like yourself couldn't see the bigger picture."

Now it was Bam's time to bark orders. "Didn't he tell you to shut the fuck up?" Her conscience was killing her. She didn't want to hear about their future together, especially when she knew he only had moments left to live. She just wished Jason would hurry up and do what he came to do.

Bam reached in and grabbed a large black duffle bag filled with cash and cocaine. She felt dirty. What was this about—Shanine and Monya, or doing a straight jux?

"OK, so y'all got what you came for . . ." Big Mike's voice trailed off. At that moment he realized he might not see another day. Were they really just gonna take his shit and bounce? Sure, he'd heard of home invasions, but normally you didn't know who set you up. These two were brazen. No masks. No remorse. No worries.

"Jay, I know you ain't gonna do me ugly over no bread, man. It's only money. I can make that shit right back. It ain't that serious."

"Nah, man. This ain't over no bread. This is for Monya

and Shanine."

Before Big Mike could plead for his life, Jason raised the barrel of his gun and put one shot in his temple, stopping his heart instantly.

The take from Big Mike was more than Cartier expected. When Bam and Jason came downstairs with two huge duffle bags and climbed in the backseat, she already knew what it was. Immediately she put the car in motion as Jason rummaged through the bags.

"Yo, we got at least four hundred large and nine keys," Jason said.

"Say word?" Cartier replied.

"Word," Bam said. "So how're we gonna break this down?"

As Jason and Cartier remained silent, Bam tried her hardest not to concentrate on the events that just happened. The hurt she heard in Big Mike's voice. The sad expression in his eyes. The sound the gun made as the bullet squeezed through the chamber. The smell of gunpowder permeating the room. The body slumped over in the chair as his head lolled to one side. The last time they made love.

Yeah, as Cartier and Jason tried to wrap their minds around Bam wanting a cut from their new retirement plan, Bam was desperately trying to clear her conscience.

Finally Cartier spoke up, "Jay, toss Bam a stack, and once we get off all the bricks, there'll be more for you. Is that cool, Bam?"

No, bitch, that ain't cool. "A'ight. Whatever."

CHAPTER 10

Old Habits Die Hard

"Don't you look sexy?" Jason took in the beauty that stood before him in all-black silk La Perla lace panties and bra set.

"All for you, *papi*," she replied in a thick Hispanic accent. "You like?"

Nodding his head vigorously, Jason inched toward his mistress and grabbed her tiny waist. His hands slowly glided down her wide, shapely hips. Everything about her was perfect in his eyes. She had white-girl dainty features and complexion, with a black girl's voluptuous body, all wrapped up in a Puerto Rican package. He couldn't ask for more.

He cupped both his hands around her juicy ass and pulled her in close, making her giggle. "Dance for me." He sat back on her bed and began to loosen his pants.

Jalissa stood back and began to gyrate her hips in a slow, seductive manner, just the way he liked it. She could see him growing hard beneath his jeans as she dipped her ass low and then came back up.

Neither one of them said a word, their eyes doing the

talking. When Jalissa knew Jason was ready for her, she climbed over and sat on his lap and began to grind her hips into his rock-hard dick.

Jason's tongue slid into Jalissa's mouth as his hands groped her firm, perky breasts. Then he began to suckle on her breast like a newborn. As Jalissa moaned with pleasure, he laid her back on her bed and slid off her panties to expose a manicured landing strip. A soft bush of hair was in front of his face as he bent down to eat her ripe pussy.

He slid his index finger in, and warm juices seeped out. He then began to flick his tongue rapidly against her clit and then slowed down to suck it, sending her over the top.

"Ahhh! Papi, you so good. Don't stop! Ahhh!"

As Jalissa sang her praises for Jason's tongue game, he was getting more and more aroused. He stood up quickly and ripped off his clothes. "Sit on my face."

Jalissa then straddled Jason and opened her pussy wide. His long tongue slid from her sweet box to her anus. She then leaned over and engulfed his bulging dick and began to suck him off until he came in her mouth. Slinking around, she crawled on top of him, because they both still wanted more, and mounted him.

Jason eased his slim penis into Jalissa's moist pussy, and they began to fuck in sync. Jason loved the way she moved her hips and dug her fingernails into his skin.

"Papi, you make me feel sooo good," she crooned.

"You love this dick, don't you?" Jason pushed deeper and deeper into her love box.

"Umm-hmm."

They both reached their climax, sweat pouring from their glistening bodies. Jalissa collapsed on top of Jason's broad, masculine chest. As she lay nestled in his strong arms, he ran his fingers through her soft hair.

"You didn't find out where Ryan live at yet from your sister?"

"She not tell. She say she not know, but I keep try, no?"

"Hell, yeah, keep trying. You see what the fuck went down last week at the club. That nigga was gunning for my head."

"I cry the whole night. No sleep. I not know if you hurt. You not call me, papi," Jalissa whined in a baby-like voice.

"Yo, I'm sorry about that shit, but something gots to give. I can't be out here hustling and looking over my shoulder for that nigga. You feel me?"

"I keep questions. You my man, but if he know, he will kill me. *Bang! Bang!*"

Jason's pressure rose at the thought of Ryan doing something to hurt Jalissa. Especially over his beef. He knew he was asking her a lot and putting her life in danger, but the circumstances were extreme.

"I will kill his whole family, including your sister, if he puts one finger on you, and that's word to my mother!"

Jalissa shook her head. "My sister not like me. She like you and Ryan. She don't play."

Jason understood what Jalissa was trying to say. Jalissa was a good girl. All she cared about was catering to her man. She wasn't a gangsta chick like Cartier, and from what she was describing, or like her sister either.

He pressed again. "That's why you gotta find out where Ryan live, so I can take care of it all."

"I will try hard, but what if something . . . uh . . . uh . . . how you say, oh, happens and I got to go bye. Run, run. I have no money. I have nothing."

With her limited English, Jason understood where she was coming from. He did give her money to buy clothes, get her hair and nails done, and pay her bills, but that was punk money. If something happened to him, if he got jammed up, and if Ryan knew she set him up, she was right; she wouldn't have any money to flee.

"A'ight, I got you. I'm gonna make sure you straight. I've been stashing bread for a while, so I could get out of the game."

"*Cuànto?* Uh, how much you save?"

"You don't need to know all of that. Just know that I'ma hit you off and you'll be straight."

Jalissa pouted. "You no trust?"

Jason tried to caress her face, but she pulled away.

"You no trust me? I trust."

Jason paused.

"OK, you're right. If I want you to trust me that I won't let anything happen to you by helping me get at Ryan, then I need to trust you as well. I got over two million saved—"

"Two million dollars?" Jalissa said, her voice elevated.

"Be easy, ma. *I* got, not *we*. You feel me?"

Jalissa nodded, poking her bottom lip out.

"But I just came off with about two hundred large. I'm going to break you off a piece of that to put in a safe place. You hear me? I don't want you to keep it here. What about your mom's house? Where she live at?"

"No, no. I not keep it there. I put it in box in bank."

Jason smiled. Maybe she wasn't as green as he thought. "Oh, you got a safety deposit box?"

Jalissa started to stroke his chest. "No, I no have no money. But I get, like the movies, no?"

"Exactly. Exactly like the movies. You go and get one tomorrow."

Before Jason left, Jalissa waited on him hand and foot. She was at his beck and call. She ran his bath and washed his whole body. She had a plush robe and fluffy slippers waiting for him. She massaged his body with warm baby oil. She made his dinner and served him his plate in bed, hopping up each time he wanted a refill of Henny or another Corona.

When morning came, he didn't have to ask her to cook breakfast, because she woke him up to breakfast. There wasn't ever any backtalk. If he told her he didn't like a specific color lip gloss on her, she immediately wiped it off and chucked the tube in the trash. Jalissa was like no other woman he'd ever fucked with, and he found himself in love way before he even knew what hit him.

"Why you treat me so good, huh?" he asked her as he ate his breakfast.

"Your wife, she not treat you this way?"

The very word *wife* and the thought of Cartier soured his stomach. He knew he was going to hear her mouth about spending the night out, but right now he wanted to enjoy his time with Jalissa.

"I don't want to talk about her right how. Just know that I like how you treat me, and that if you want to keep me around, keep doing what you're doing."

Jalissa smiled sweetly and gave him a succulent kiss on his lips. "You my *rey*, means *king* in *Español*. I do, umm, treat you good."

❦

Cartier wasn't sure exactly when Jason had moved all their money from their safe. Not only was their life savings gone, but also the money they'd scored from Big Mike. She decided to wake him up and ask him.

"Jay. Jay, get up," Cartier gave Jason a strong nudge.

When he opened his eyes, she sat down on the bed beside him. "I just went to get some pocket money from the safe and also give Bam another grip, because she keep beefin', but it ain't there. The drugs are still there, but all our money is gone."

"What the fuck Bam beefin' 'bout?"

"You know, she feels like she could get a bigger cut because, if it wasn't for her, she feels we wouldn't have the money, nor would we have gotten rid of one of our enemies."

"Yo, that bitch is buggin'! She act like she put in the work. That was all me, and now she want a bigger handout?

Get the fuck outta here! When I see Bam, I swear I'ma put my foot in her ass! I swear, that's a dumb-ass bitch!"

"Why you yellin' and actin' all stupid? There's more than enough to go around. We could toss her another ten." Cartier shook her head at her own greed. "In fact, Jay, this just occurred to me. We have to divide the take three ways. Bam deserves more than the ten grand I just mentioned. She had feelings for him, and what we made her do isn't really sitting well with me these days. You know I can be hotheaded. I react first, and then think later. I keep thinking, what if Big Mike really didn't have anything to do with it? And what about Bam's feelings? I haven't heard from her these past few weeks, other than to ask for more bread, and I want—I *need* to mend our friendship."

Jason couldn't believe Cartier's hypocrisy. Now she feels bad after duke is dead and buried? What about that night when she was barking orders? He'd told her that he'd do it all by himself, but no, she *made* Bam participate. Now she wants to wake him up out of his peaceful sleep with this epic saga about Bam, that's supposed to tug at his heartstrings.

"Yo, what's this about? Is this about you feeling bad about Big Mike being laid to rest, or is this about you just wanting to kick it with Bam?"

Cartier didn't understand the question. "It's about both."

"Stop lying! This me you talkin' to. You don't give a fuck about Big Mike. Nor do you give a fuck that Bam had to witness me putting a bullet in his head. All you care about is that Bam ain't around to gossip with you, or go get that doobie hair wrap— whatever you girls call it— anymore, and now you want to buy back her friendship!"

"That's not true."

"Whatever." Jason turned back over and pulled the covers over his head.

Cartier refused to leave. "Well, I don't care what you think my motivation is, but the fact still remains that Bam needs more money. That's the right thing to do. Shit, we didn't even move all those keys. That's at least another two hundred. As far as I'm concerned, that's free money, so we don't have to be greedy."

Jason sat straight up. "Ain't shit about that money free!" He couldn't believe his ears. Jalissa was going against her own blood for him, and here, Cartier was taking up for a friend. "That money got twenty-five to life written all over it, and I'll be damned if I'm giving Bam another muthafuckin' dime. I'm telling you, Cartier, you better check your friend, 'fore they find her silly ass floating in the Hudson River."

"Jason, you're working my nerves, and it's just nine o'clock in the morning. Bam ain't just a chick off the street. She's already proven herself to us for what she did to her man, and honestly, if I were in her shoes, I can't say it would have played out the same way. So I don't care how you feel about the situation. Bam deserves more. So, where's the money?"

"I needed it to buy some work."

Cartier thought quickly. Did this muthafucka just say he took the money to buy work, when there's a safe full of drugs that ain't even sold yet?

She began slowly. "Some work?" Although she wanted to flip, she was going to be calm for once in her life, until she found out what was really going on. "Ain't there enough work in the closet?"

"Look, stop questioning me! I'm fuckin' moving heroin now, not just coke. I took the fuckin' money—all of it—to handle my business, and Bam ain't getting shit. When I'm done, we're going to be set for life. I'm talking like a six- or seven-million-dollar return. Now, can you go and make yourself useful? A nigga hungry. Can you go and make me breakfast?"

"Eat your muthafuckin' fingers, bitch!" Cartier yelled, and stormed out of their bedroom.

Jason just shook his head. He knew where he could get a good meal.

❧

It had been weeks since Cartier's and Jason's last argument, and months since they'd made love. As the realization hit Cartier, she couldn't understand why she felt threatened. That night she made a delicious meal and called Jason and asked him to come home early for dinner. She put on the new lingerie from Victoria's Secret, flattering in color and texture. But as the hours slipped from early evening to the wee hours of the morning, she knew he was up to his old ways.

Cartier awoke in the morning with puffy eyes from crying herself to sleep, to a husband that reeked of alcohol. She didn't know what to do or say, but she didn't want another screaming match. And she missed Jason so much.

She moved closer to him and began to massage his penis until it got erect. Groggily he opened his eyes and pushed her away.

"But I want you," Cartier said. "Let's make love."

Jason pretended he didn't hear her as he fell back to sleep on his stomach.

For months Bam probably got less than four hours of sleep each night. The grief assassin would haunt her dreams with visions of Big Mike's murder. Within a matter of hours, her future with Big Mike had gone up in a mushroom cloud, and Bam couldn't put her finger on how it took that turn for the worse. What could she have done differently to get a different outcome? Should she have told Big Mike that he was suspected of killing her friends and to watch his back? All he thought was that he was supplying information for them to get Ryan. Selfishly, Bam didn't want to reveal that because she knew he wouldn't come near her with a ten-foot pole, and he would have been justified.

Should she have told Jason to fuck off and taken her chances that he was bluffing? Would Jason have really pulled the trigger on her?

Besides, would Cartier have allowed Jason to pull the trigger on her? Today, Bam still couldn't answer that.

Every night the loud, thunder-like blast from Jason's .357 would jolt Bam out of her sleep. Drenched in sweat, she would get up and walk around her apartment, clicking on televisions and lights.

She'd gone to the doctor, who'd prescribed Ambien to help her sleep, but when she complained that the maximum 4-mg dosage wasn't working, he told her she could be suffering from depression, and recommended a therapist.

Bam laughed in his face. *What could a therapist say to undo Big Mike's murder?*

The doctor said, "Bernice, sometimes in life you can't choose your path, but you can choose how you walk it. There isn't anything wrong with going to see a therapist. It could possibly make your walk in life a little less cumbersome. Think about it."

Bam didn't want to think about it. She knew her life was a series of perfect storms, and just as she'd gotten through ugly events in the past, she'd get past this too.

❧

At first, Cartier wanted to deflect her problems with her husband, but now she was at the breaking point. It was early April, and a random rainstorm came roaring through New York. Cartier was trapped in the house, sitting on her terrace, watching the waves hit the shore. Instead of living her best life now, appreciating her new home, healthy kids, and the fact that she and Li'l Momma had mended their friendship and were on better terms than ever before, wasn't enough.

Cartier wanted it all. She wanted a strong marriage and her friend back. Slowly, she and Bam had begun talking again, but it wasn't the same. Cartier knew it would take time. Every time she asked Bam to go with her to Sophie's, she would have an excuse.

Jason had resorted to not coming home two, three nights a week, and all the arguing and fighting couldn't get him to stop being so disrespectful. There was always an excuse the next day when he'd come home. He'd either fallen asleep at Wonderful's house, too drunk to come home, or was so wrapped up in a drug deal that he couldn't stop to call her and tell her that he'd be out all night. Or— and Cartier couldn't believe he'd said this one—he just needed alone time and copped a hotel room all by himself just to think. The laundry list of excuses was growing.

Cartier kicked him out, tossing his clothes on the front lawn. He gladly loaded them into his car and didn't dial her one time begging to come home. This didn't go unnoticed by Cartier. Her mother's wise words would resonate through her head continually.

"Don't kick him out, Cartier," she'd said, "unless you're really ready for him to go. Because, I promise you, there's a woman out there with her door wide open just waiting to pick up where you left off. Now, if you're ready to move on, then kick him to the curb and start your life over. But if you're doing it to make a statement, or get a reaction, you might not like what he dishes back at you."

When Trina had said those words to Cartier, it went in one ear and out the next. In a blind rage, Cartier kicked him out, and it was barely forty-eight hours later before she wanted him back. She couldn't understand why, or how. All she knew was that she did. When he didn't call, she got physically sick. She wanted to know who he was messing around with, and why wasn't he kissing her butt to come back home.

She called Bam. "Bam, listen, I know things are strained between us, but I really need you right now."

"Cartier, I was just about to head out. Could I call you back?"

Cartier knew she could go downstairs and talk to Trina, but she didn't want motherly wisdom; she wanted to kick it with females her own age, friends who were there from the beginning. She knew she could call Li'l Momma, but Bam was always there for her, from the get-go.

When Jason was stepping out on her with Monya, Bam held Cartier down. She made her feel better while she suffered in silence in a prison cell. So, if anyone knew how Cartier truly felt about Jason, it was Bam.

"Jason is cheating again," Cartier blurted out, and her voice broke. As tears began to gush down her cheeks, Cartier couldn't believe she was breaking down so quickly and openly. "I don't know what I'll do if I catch him cheating again."

At first Bam wondered if this was a ploy to put their friendship back on track. But when she heard Cartier sobbing from the other end, she knew this was real.

"Why you think that?"

"Actually I know it! I kicked him out of the house weeks ago, and he hasn't as much as called me to see how the kids are doing."

"So he hasn't been home in weeks?"

"Nope. He's been acting differently, and I promise you, Bam, whoever she is, she means a lot to him."

"What? Why are you crying? I know you not lettin' no chick trump you. You've dealt with Jason cheating before, Cartier, and you know as I do, he always comes back home to you. There ain't a girl out there that could hold his heart. He's just being stubborn."

"It's not that I'm folding. I'm telling you that this time it's different. I don't know who she is, but Jason wasn't touching me anymore. He was grumpy all the time, and whenever I would ask him a question, any question, he was flipping on me. That's not Jason . . . not the Jason I fell in love with."

"You sure it's not this beef? Maybe he has a lot on his mind."

"It's not just his beef, Bam. It's our beef, and he's not the only one who's affected. So I know that's not it. I'm telling you, he's seeing someone."

Bam walked to her refrigerator and pulled out a bottle of Moscato wine. It was barely ten o'clock in the morning. She poured her breakfast. "Well, if I were you, I'd call him and tell him you want him to come home."

"I can't do that," Cartier said weakly, although that's exactly what she wanted to do. "I'd play myself, right?"

Bam took a large gulp. "You're his wife. Who the fuck cares? In relationships we're supposed to play ourselves for the one we love here and there. You've already proven your point by kicking him out. Now his playtime is over. Don't allow him to be a free agent out there for too long to really get attached to anyone. I think that would be a big mistake. And a few weeks, in my opinion, is giving some chick too much wifey time."

"You haven't heard anything on the streets?"

"If I did, I'm not sure I would tell you."

"What do you mean by that?"

"The last thing I confided in you got me involved in a murder, and my man assassinated!"

Cartier took the low blow like a champ. She knew it would take a long time for Bam to fully get over what happened to Big Mike, but right now her marriage was on the line, and she wanted Bam to be her sister girl, not some bitter chick ready to rehash something that couldn't be undone.

"Bam, I know it'll take you a while to understand where my head was at, but if Shanine and Monya could be here, they'd tell you that you did the right thing."

"How do you know what they'd say? What gives you the authority to speak for the dead?" Bam said, her voice laced with anger.

"You know what? You're right. I can't speak for them, nor can I undo what's already been done. Once that trigger was pulled, it was like a bell ringing. It couldn't be unrung. I've already apologized, Bam. I don't know what else I can say."

"But had you only listened to me, then we wouldn't have to have this conversation. If you had just trusted me and my instincts, Big Mike wouldn't be dead."

"Bam, let me make this clear for this one last time. I'm not saying, nor will I ever say, that Big Mike was blameless. We won't ever be able to know that with certainty. The only people who truly know what happened aren't talking or aren't able to talk." Cartier paused. She didn't want to say anything to jeopardize the road back to friendship, but she couldn't allow Bam to think they had killed an innocent man. "But you keep bringing this up as if I could fix it like I fix my hair, and that won't ever happen. It's done, and we have to live with it and, hopefully, get past this together. I need you, Bam. And I hope you need me in your life too."

Bam wasn't ready to answer that, so she walked the conversation back around the block. "So, what are you going to do about Jason? Are you going to just let him keep cheating on you?"

"Well, right now it's only speculation. I don't really know for sure that he's cheating. I just got a feeling."

"And we all know that our feelings, a woman's intuition, will never steer us wrong. So, you know he's cheating. You can either give him a call and tell him to come home, or file for divorce."

"I don't just want to throw him away."

"Well, then you've solved your own dilemma. Get to dialing."

Cartier could tell Bam was ready to end the conversation, but she wanted to hold on to each moment and make it last longer. "I do want to put the spark back in our marriage."

"Girl, you know how to seduce a man. Cook him a nice dinner and suck his dick. And don't forget to swallow the cum. Get frisky, chick. Men love a freak."

Cartier laughed slightly. *If it was only that easy*, she thought. "Maybe we could go away where there won't be any distractions, and we could maybe renew our vows or something. Maybe run to Vegas for a few days. Truthfully, I've always wanted to get married, for real, for real. Like not behind bars, you know, all the whispers behind the scenes from bitches saying that getting married while locked down wasn't the real deal. What do you think, Bam?"

"I think that's hot. He'll love it. And while you're planning your trip, I'll keep my ears to the street to see if I hear anything." Bam was ready to agree with anything at that moment. She'd already tossed back half the bottle of wine and had gotten bored with Cartier's conversation. Why should she be excited about weddings and vacations when she could have been making the same plans?

"You'd do that for me?"

"You know you're my girl."

Finding out who Jason was sleeping with was the last thing on Bam's to-do list. Besides, Jason had scads of women. It would probably have been easier to name who he wasn't sleeping with.

Bam laughed at her own thoughts and crawled back into her bed to cry her eyes out.

～∞〇～

That night Cartier decided to take Bam's advice by swallowing her pride and asking Jason to come back home. Her heart palpitated from fear as she dialed his number and throughout each ring. When he allowed her call to go to voicemail she was consumed with an overwhelming sense of hopelessness. Was it really over? Had she finally taken it too far? Was she systematically losing everyone she loved most?

After downing a half bottle of Patrón and pineapple juice, Cartier was violently shaken out of her drunken stupor by Jason.

"I see you been missing a nigga . . ."

CHAPTER 11

Unthinkable

As May rolled around, the weather was just beginning to dry out from the April showers when Cartier got the phone call she was dreading. Janet called the house to say that Monya had taken a turn for the worse, and the ventilators were no longer able to sustain her heart and brain. The doctors said she probably wouldn't make it through the night.

"This can't happen," Cartier said in disbelief. "I thought she would get better."

Janet was tired and weary. "She's ready to go, Cartier. As much as it pains me to say this, my baby wants to be at rest. She's a fighter, and she's fighting being here. I'm calling to tell everyone to go to the hospital to say their good-byes."

❧

The beeps from the ventilator could be heard from the opposite end of the hallway. The smell of death, antiseptics, and dried blood from the ICU assaulted Cartier's nostrils as soon as she stepped out of the elevator. When she arrived no one was there with her friend. Her body lay still, as if already dead, in the small twin bed. Her already slender frame was emaciated and hardly visible underneath the sheer white hospital sheet. Instantly Cartier burst into tears and collapsed at Monya's bedside.

Thirty minutes later she was still in tears. She just couldn't bear to let her go.

"We got one of them," Cartier managed to say. Laced with regret and grief, her own voice sounded foreign to her. Up until now, she didn't feel a need to tell Monya anything but good, positive things. "Big Mike . . . he's gone, Monya. And I promise you that we'll get Ryan too."

Cartier wiped her tears and then looked at her best friend. Her eyes were tightly shut, a tube assisting her breathing. "Monya, you're still beautiful." Cartier's voice got stronger as she reminisced. "I would never tell you this in the past, but you were always the prettiest out of our crew. I bet you knew that, didn't you? You thought you were hot shit."

Cartier laughed somewhat. "In fact, we all thought we were the shit. You couldn't tell us nothing. Remember when we boosted those mink coats"—Another hearty laugh. "Baby, our names were ringing bells. We were the youngest bitches to come through with mink coats and stilettos. Those were the good days."

Cartier looked off, through the window, her voice beginning to crack. "We sure did have fun back then. Back when we didn't think our actions had consequences."

She reached down and grabbed Monya's hand. It was ice-cold. "Monya, I know you're tired of being here, and you're ready to go." Once again her voice choked up. "I want you to know that we're taking real good care of Jason Jr., and he'll be raised in a loving home. I'll always share great stories about you with him. He'll definitely know his mother through me. Oh, and before I forget—"

The loud beeping jolted Cartier's thoughts. She couldn't remember what she was about to say. Everything happened so fast. One moment she heard a CODE BLUE announcement, the next, she was being ushered out of the way by a doctor and two nurses. She watched in horror as a team of professionals worked on her friend. Using the defibrillator, they tried to jump-start Monya's heart. Less than five minutes later, Monya was gone. Just like that. Her best friend was dead, for real this time.

CHAPTER 12

Ring The Alarm

Cartier hated to feel this way, but she almost wished that Monya had passed away the same day last year as Shanine. She just couldn't stomach going to another funeral. It was all too traumatic.

"You almost ready?" Trina asked as she walked into Cartier's room. Jason and the kids were waiting for her downstairs.

"I guess."

"Well, come on now. We don't want to be late."

"Ma, it's just not fair."

"We know that already, Cartier, but there's nothing either one of us can do. So come on now. Monya is expecting you to send her off."

After the funeral everyone headed to back to their old block for an old-fashioned block party in celebration of Monya's life. People from all boroughs pulled up in droves. The Cartel had spent well over ten thousand dollars on food to feed hundreds of people; steak, turkey burgers, franks, lobster, and shrimp were all tossed on grills. Champagne arrived by the caseload—Moët, Clique, Dom P, and Piper were being crated out of Range Rovers and Cayennes. Get-money dudes rolled up with liters of Hennessy, Cîroc vodka, and Rémy. Chicks pulled up with trays full of potato salad, deviled eggs, tossed salad, and watermelons.

DJ Klue began spinning all the vintage hits, from Total, the "No One Else" remix with Lil' Kim, Foxy Brown, and Da Brat, to U.T.F.O.'s "Roxanne, Roxanne." Everyone was losing their minds, dancing on top of hooptie cars and their front stoop just celebrating.

DJ Klue put on Brandy's song "Best Friend." He said, "This song goes out to Cartier, Li'l Momma, and Bam. I see you! From Shanine and Monya. They still watching over y'all."

Everyone erupted in cheers. Cartier's grin was as wide as a slice of watermelon. She, Bam, and Li'l Momma all embraced, and they got strong encouragement from the crowd.

Later that night, everyone ended up at Janet's house looking through a stack of old photos, laughing, crying, and just reminiscing on the past. That night everyone slept over, either because they were too drunk to drive, too tired to walk, or just because they felt peaceful being around those who loved them and just wanted to enjoy the moment while it lasted.

⸎

"Where you at?" Bam asked Cartier.

"I'm home. Why?"

"You alone, or is Jason there too?"

Cartier knew Bam had dirt. She could hear the urgency in her voice and was eager for her to share. "No, no, Jason ain't here. He's running the street. What happened?"

"This ain't good, so I'm just going to give it to you straight, no chaser. I found out who Jason's fucking with, and you ain't gonna like it one bit."

Cartier's heart plummeted. Although her intuition told her Jason was fucking around, deep down inside, she was hoping she was wrong.

"Who is she?"

"Her name is Jalissa, a Puerto Rican bitch. I'm not really sure you know her, but you can find her at Sophie's any Friday of the month. And, Cartier?"

"What?"

"Her and her sister Marisol both have something in common with you. Y'all have the same taste in men. Her sister is Ryan's baby momma."

The news hit Cartier like an unstoppable force. It was wrong on so many levels. More than ten years later, she just couldn't get past Ryan leaving her to rot in jail while he hooked up with Marisol, and now to hear that her husband was fucking with the sister was beyond hurtful. She was humiliated, angered, and jealous.

"Are you positive?"

"Yeah, girl, I am. I heard it from more than once source. But the most trusted informant was Mesha, that young booster from Harlem. She said she ran into Jason in front of Bloomingdales with Jalissa last week and he bought a bag full of stolen merchandise off of her for Jalissa. She said they were all hugged up like two love birds. So what are you gonna do? I can come with you when you put your foot in her ass for fucking with your husband, but just so you know, if you fuck with Jalissa, her sister Marisol ain't gonna take shit lightly. I heard her hand-play is nice and that she keeps a .357 on her at all times. I know you ain't no punk, but I just want you to know what you're up against."

Cartier tuned Bam out as she droned on and on. She didn't have a clue about how to handle the situation. Should she confront Jason and listen to his lies? Should she run up on Jalissa and have it play out as it did with Mari back in California? Should she just kick Jason out for the last time and give up on her marriage?

"How does she look?"

"Huh?"

"Jalissa. Describe her."

"Umm, she's about our height, light skin, long brown hair with blond highlights. I dunno. She's pretty, I guess. Oh, and she has a mole next to her upper lip."

"Like Cindy Crawford?"

"Yeah, just like that."

"I know exactly who that bitch is," Cartier said, visions of the girl inside the salon flashing before her eyes. "I saw her at Sophie's the day Li'l Momma and I got into it, and I also saw her and Jason the night of the shootout in the club."

"See, didn't I tell you she went to Sophie's? So do you think she know who you are?"

"Of course, that bitch know I'm Jason's wife. She was clocking my every move in the salon. Li'l Momma checked her, but I just brushed it off. You see how sneaky these bitches are? She sat a few feet from me, just staring at me, knowing she's fucking my husband."

Bam listened to Cartier's tantrum for a few more moments before she got to the good part—the meat and potatoes as her foster mother would say.

"But check it. We gotta talk about how Jason has gone against the grain. You know I can't let this go, Cartier. Big Mike was my man, and he's dead. There's no coming back from that. Now we find out that Jason is fucking with a bitch who has ties to one of the men who murdered our friends. How are you gonna handle *that*? Because nobody gets a pass."

Cartier wondered if for the next sixty years she'd have to hear Bam bring up Big Mike. Her constantly talking about Big Mike was like hearing nails on a chalkboard; that irritating. She wished she'd just get over it already.

"I hear you, and trust, nobody's getting away with anything. I'ma handle this situation. I don't know how, but I will."

Cartier felt betrayed, and as the pieces of the puzzle began to come together, she no longer knew who to trust. What the fuck was Jason doing fucking with the enemy? Out of all the pussy in this town, why would he even go there? And how could he have been so righteous in flipping on Bam for fucking Big Mike then turn around and do the same thing? What if this chick was a double agent? What if Ryan and Jason had squashed the beef? And where was all the money they'd saved up and also scored from Big Mike? Why had Jason taken it from the house? In fact, Cartier no longer had any access to "their" money. She realized Jason was setting up to move on without her. That had to be the reason why he'd taken all of the money.

Cartier decided Trina was the only person who could give her guidance and wisdom. She went downstairs to her room.

"Ma, we need to talk, and this is some serious shit. So you gotta cut off *Grey's Anatomy* and pay attention."

Trina looked up, annoyed. Until she saw the look in her daughter's eyes. She muted the television and sat up.

"Well, if it's going to be one of those conversations, go in the kitchen and grab me one of Jason's Coronas."

Quickly, Cartier ran into the kitchen and grabbed two beers and returned to her mother. Both women cracked open the beers, and Trina waited impatiently for Cartier to get on with the story.

"I don't know where to begin, but here goes. I told you that the same night we went to the New Year's Eve party, we got into a shootout with Ryan."

"Yeah, you said that somebody set y'all up because he knew that y'all were there."

"Well, I left out that I saw Jason briefly with this

Spanish chick but didn't really think anything of it."

"So he's fucking around again, huh?"

Cartier didn't like that Trina said it so casually, as if it was to be expected. "Yeah, but this time a lot is at stake. Jason is fucking this bitch who is the sister of Ryan's baby momma."

"What?" Trina jumped up off the bed, and got really animated. "I know you didn't say he's fucking with the enemy. Is he stupid or stupid?"

"Not only that, Ma. He's been acting really distant ever since I let him come back home. We're more roommates than husband and wife, if you feel me."

Cartier didn't want to go into sexual details with her mother, but Trina got the point.

"What if this bitch sets him up with Ryan?"

Trina shook her head. "Damn! I didn't know Jason was that gullible over a piece of twat, but shit shouldn't surprise either one of us, if he was able to fuck around with your best friend. And I don't mean to hurt you by bringing it up, but it's the truth. And what his stupid ass doesn't realize is that all our lives are in danger, including the kids'. We're sitting ducks. What if this bitch has Ryan follow Jason one night on his way home? Shit, they could have already done that. What if they've found out where we live? They could run up in here and do a home invasion and murder us all."

"Those are my thoughts as well. What if this chick is the one who told Ryan that Jason would be at the club that night? And here we were suspecting Bam. And you know his whipped ass ain't even suspect that possibility, because he's still fucking with her."

"I just want to know how this happened."

"I don't give a fuck about the how, or truthfully, the why. The point is, he violated, and he should be held accountable."

"Well, if you're asking my advice, I'm going to tell you not to bring it up or begin to show that you're jealous. If a man think that another chick has your pressure up, he'll immediately put that chick on a pedestal."

"I got to do something."

"Jason is a good provider and a good father. He'll see the error in his ways, and he'll cut that bitch off. She don't mean nothing to him. Trust me."

"Ya think, huh? You think you know Jason. Well, know that Jason snuck all of our money out of this house, and if shit hit the fan today or tomorrow, you and I are back to Brooklyn in a heartbeat."

"What do you mean, he took all the money?"

"I've been on him since we came back from Los Angeles to save money for a rainy day, and he was doing that. He'd saved close to at least a million dollars, and then we got that score from Big Mike, and money just kept rolling in. He was approaching our retirement goal quickly, and then one day I go to the safe and all the bread is gone and he has this lame excuse. Now I don't know where the money is at, and he is basically telling me to kick rocks. No matter how much I curse him out about the money, he just screams back."

This new information was disturbing to Trina. She knew men kept their money with their loved ones. And if it wasn't in this house or at least where Cartier could get her hands on to it, then she was right—Jason was most likely open off this new bitch. Trina felt that her daughter had gone through too much to be left broke. That wasn't going to happen.

"So Jason not only walked out of here with over a million dollars and you don't have one coin to even bail his stupid ass out if he got jammed up, but he's also fucking with a Spanish chick whose sister is the mother of Ryan's child. And chances are that she could now be the keeper of all that cash? Oh, hells no! No fucking way is this Spanish bitch and that little-dick muthafucka gonna get over on my daughter." Trina's mind was spinning with thoughts. She knew if the feds kicked in the front door, the house held a hefty mortgage, and that even if she and Cartier both got jobs, they couldn't afford it. So that meant that Cartier needed a stash for rainy days, which, when you're in the drug game, were sure to happen.

"Where's the drugs y'all scored from Big Mike?"

"The drugs? They still here. With what we took off Mike, and from Jason's stash, there's eleven keys."

Trina reached for her Newport and lit it. "You know, first off, there shouldn't be any muthafuckin' drugs up in here, with these kids, but I didn't wanna say anything 'cause this ain't really my crib. But fuck all of that. That little dirty bastard gonna leave us up in here dirty while he toss all that cash toward a new bitch, and you been down with him for how long? You the mother of his kid! This shit is unbelievable! So how much that tally to?" Trina took a moment to calculate the street value of the drugs. "OK, so that's like two, three hundred large, give or take."

"Yeah. So?"

"So? So we're gonna rob him."

Cartier's eyes popped open wide like she was spooked. "Come again?"

"When he leaves the house tomorrow morning, you're going to move all that shit to my apartment in Brooklyn. He doesn't have a key. Then you'll call him and tell him that we're going to Shanine and Monya's grave. Before we leave, we'll break a window and toss a few things around. Call him around eight o'clock and tell him we've been robbed. Make it sound good, Cartier. Jason can't catch on that we set him up. Ask him, did he tell anybody where we lived over and over again. Make him start thinking twice about this new bitch. Ask, could anybody have followed him leaving any destinations. You feel me?"

Cartier's grin said it all.

Trina continued. "You still got your connections to move the weight?"

"No doubt."

"Good. In a couple months, get The Cartel back together and begin unloading those keys. Ain't no way my baby ain't gonna have a cash flow. And while you're at it, you better start bleeding Jason dry. Run his pockets every night he comes home drunk and stash half of his pocket money. Let him buy you jewelry and pretend to lose it. Get robbed, whatever excuse you can think of, and in the meantime, don't ever mention this new bitch. But, Cartier?"

"Yes."

"I want you to be extra careful out on these streets. I don't want to lose you like Janet lost Monya. Don't leave the house without your piece. Always look in your mirrors when you're on your way home, and always circle the block before you open up the garage, you know, shit like that. I don't know what's going on, but something is going to go down, and I will go postal if I lose you."

Cartier would take Trina's advice, but she couldn't agree to turning the other cheek about Jason and his new affair. She promised Jason that if he ever cheated on her again, she'd fuck him and his mistress up. Thinking logically, Cartier knew that if she gave Jalissa a fair one and kicked her ass, she'd have to look over her shoulders forever to see who would be coming at her. Not that she was afraid. Hardly. But she did have the kids to think about, and bitches running up on you while you're with your kids in Wal-Mart ain't something to look forward to.

Cartier realized she had to take care of not only Jalissa but Marisol too, and she couldn't help but keep Ryan at the top of the list.

❧

"Yo, our house just got robbed!" Cartier screamed frantically to the unsuspecting Jason.

"What the fuck you mean?"

"Trina and us just got back from the cemetery, and someone came through and robbed us! They took the whole safe. They got everything. Did you ever put that money back?"

"What money?"

"Our money. That money we've been saving. Did you ever put the re-up money back, once you came off with that heroin?"

"Aw, man! Yeah, I just put back the money last night," Jason lied.

"Damn, Jay! I was hoping you didn't put the money back." Cartier began to cry, amazed her acting was that good. "Now what are we gonna do?"

"Don't worry. I'll be home soon."

"No!" Cartier yelled. "The police are on their way to investigate. I don't want you around those peoples."

"Then why the fuck did you call them? You know they got a good nose and can sniff out a hustler. You and Trina will stick out like sore thumbs."

"We didn't call the police, the neighbor did. They saw a group of Hispanic men rushing from out of our house, holding heavy things, and knew it didn't look right, so they called the police."

"A group of Hispanic men?"

"Yeah, that's what I said. I've been wracking my brain, trying to figure out who the fuck could have found out where we live. Bam and Li'l Momma have never been here, and I always make sure I'm not being followed. What about you?"

"What about me?"

"Can you think of anyone who could have followed you home on one of your drunk nights, or maybe did you slip up and tell someone where we lived?"

"You talking crazy now. I ain't never got caught slippin'. This just some random shit."

"Random? Thieves got away with all of our money, and the package, and it's just random? What are we going to do for money now?"

"Cartier, please stop nagging me. Haven't I always taken care of you? This is a little setback, but bills will be paid at the beginning of each month."

I know they will, bitch! Because you still got all our money stashed away with your slut!

"OK. I'll see you when you get home. I'm going to talk to the police, clean up, and then put the kids to bed."

"OK, cool."

"Love you."

"I'll see you later. One."

When Jason came home the next day, he was pissed, as well as leery. He didn't have a clue about who could have robbed his crib, but he was relieved that he'd removed the money. Home invasions happened all the time in the drug game, but that usually ended with the drug dealer and his family's brains being splattered all over their marble floors. This was more of a robbery. Get in and get out type of MO. Burglars target high-end neighborhoods all the time expecting to score family heirlooms and expensive paintings. Maybe it was all coincidental and had nothing to do with them.

With everyone shook up, Jason decided to hire a security company to install top-of-the-line equipment. There wasn't any way he'd be a sitting mark, nor would he allow anyone to harm a hair on his kids' heads.

Ten thousand dollars and five hours later, he couldn't stop grinning at his new toy. He couldn't help but feel like Al Pacino in *Scarface*. Their bedroom and Trina's bedroom had eight monitors installed that gave real-time footage of the garage, and ten cameras facing every angle of the house.

There wasn't any way anyone could approach the house without them being aware of it. And when Jason or Cartier wasn't available to watch, then Trina would be watching too as she watched her soap operas.

A cellular backup GPS device was added to the existing alarm system, so even if someone cut the telephone line hooked to the system, the backup system would automatically kick in. They even added a sensor on the ceilings so that if someone broke a window to avoid being detected by the motion sensor, the glass sensor would automatically kick in and set off the alarm.

As Jason sat, grinning like the cat that ate the canary, Cartier asked, "What are you grinning about?"

"Huh?" he asked, suddenly feeling foolish.

"I said, what the fuck are you grinning about? Did you forget we just got robbed? Not only for the coke, but all of our money."

Jason had almost forgotten the lie about the money being put back. They were supposed to be broke, and not really having a coin to their name.

"I'm smiling because I'm taking measures to protect my family. Am I wrong to feel good about that?"

"Jay, money is the best protection your family could have, and we don't have a dime. Where's our mortgage protection? Our car note protection? Our light, water, and gas bill protection? Huh? How 'bout that?"

"You can't even stop for one second to thank God that when those peoples ran up in here you or the kids weren't here. All you can ever talk about is that gwap! I told you that you don't got shit to worry about. I've always taken care of my family, and this setback won't stop my flow. I got some shit working in the pipeline, and I assure you, we gonna be straight again."

Cartier knew he was lying. She could barely look at his face. How could he take their money and cut her out and feel good about that? Cartier knew, though, it wasn't who won the battle, but who won the war. Jason might think he'd gotten over, but she planned to be the last chick standing, whatever that meant and whatever the cost.

CHAPTER 13

The Art of War

The two sultry women loved to get together and plot. As far as they were concerned, they were smarter and prettier than any chick and more cut-throat and heartless than any nigga. In other words, a person's worst nightmare would materialize if they ever found themselves on the wrong side of the fence with either one of these sisters.

"OK, so where are we with Jason? Did he bring you the money to hold yet?"

"Nah, he still acting shook, but I'ma break him in a few more weeks. I'll put my life on that. That nigga pussy-whipped."

"So, what's taking so long? You should have that by now. I'm already spending that fuckin' dough in my head."

"You know what? I had him. I had him ready to bring me the money to put in my box, but then something happened. I don't know what. He won't tell me, but something must have gone down that spooked him. But it won't take long before I get him back into his good graces. And the sooner, the better. I'm so tired of pretending that me speaka very little English."

Both girls erupted in laughter.

"Shit. I know we're Puerto Rican, but we were born in Brooklyn, not Puerto Rico, and none of our family speak Spanish. I can't even understand that shit. Sometimes, I be saying words I got off the Internet just moments before he walks through the door."

"He's one dumb muthafucka!" Marisol added.

"He's one of the easiest marks we ever ran. All he wants is a subservient bitch. When he's in my crib, I feel like an indentured servant, running all over the apartment, fixing him shit, grabbing him beers, picking up his funky clothes." Jalissa rolled her eyes. "And after all of that, I gotta fuck him and suck his little dick and act like I like it. Oh, please believe me when I tell you that I'll have the money within the next two weeks, or I promise, I will put a bullet in his head myself and save Ryan the hassle."

Marisol walked to the mirror on the armoire and began to brush her silky hair. Then she reapplied her lip gloss. She was going out to dinner with her boo tonight.

"You know, we gotta wrap this shit up quickly. If Ryan finds out you're fucking with Jason, he'll kill you. And then I'll have to kill him, and that won't be a good look."

Jalissa nodded. "I know. But we're both careful. I sure as hell don't want Ryan to find out, and he sure as hell don't want his wife to find out. So I think we're good."

"Speaking of wifey, she could be a problem too, if things hit the streets. I heard she did a bid for a murder."

"That bitch can't fuck with you! Jason already pulled her card and said she did the bid for her homegirl. Some chick that was down with her crew was the one who put in the work; one of the same chicks Ryan got that big score from."

Marisol remained quiet for a while. She knew more about The Cartel than she was letting on. Ryan ran his mouth for years about Cartier being thorough, and although she might not have been the one to kill that local drug hustler, she was there, and she had the heart to actually do the bid. That spoke volumes in Marisol's book.

"I know that bitch can't fuck with me, but I don't sleep on anyone. Jalissa, always remember, anyone could get got. Even me. So don't ever let your guards down. We're playing a dangerous game, and as always, we gotta be smart so we can't get sloppy. We have to stick to the plan, which is drain Jason for all of his money, and then give me the information to feed to Ryan to dead him. And although we're not losing any sleep over his bitch, it would be better that she never find out about y'all, because that would cause unnecessary drama. Remember, this isn't about beef. This is about getting paid. Going to war with his wife won't bring a dime into either one of our pockets.

"Now Ryan, on the other hand, is a different story. For money, he inherited a beef. He killed those girls to bring money into our household, and now Jason feels as though he has to step in and be a superhero to seek revenge. When he feels those hot slugs enter his body, he'll wish he had rethought his decision to fuck with my boo. You know"—Marisol paused and turned to face Jalissa—"People out here think Ryan is soft like butter, like he just a pretty boy and he don't hold shit down. But ain't nothing soft about my baby. He hard, from his block head to his rock-hard dick."

Marisol blushed at the thought of making love to her man. They were connected mentally and sexually, and she loved it.

"I'm ready." Jalissa stood before Marisol. "And hurry up, because Jason is coming over tonight. I still got to run home and cook, douche, you know, all that good shit."

Marisol exhaled. "Are you sure this is necessary?"

"Marisol, you said it yourself that we gotta stick to the plan. Well, this is part of the new plan, and I'm sticking to it. That nigga said he got over two million dollars in the stash, so this is worth it. It's just a little insurance on my part so that he'll continue to trust me if I show him my allegiance."

Marisol let out a little giggle. "Now we both know that if he said he got two million then he got half that. You know how niggas lie."

"Well, however much he got, it's more than what I got, so go ahead. Do it!"

Marisol pulled her fist way back and then let it go.

Immediately Jalissa's hands both went up and clutched her right eye as she doubled over in pain. "Awww, shit. That fucking hurt." She felt her eye swell up.

"Let me see it." Marisol squinted to see the damage.

Just as both girls had hoped, Jalissa's eye was almost swollen shut.

"It's perfect."

❦

When Jalissa opened up her front door and Jason saw her face, he went beserk. "What the fuck happened to you?"

Immediately his mind thought crazy thoughts. He didn't know if Cartier had found out he was cheating and whipped her ass, which wouldn't have been a stretch for Cartier.

Jalissa put her head down and walked farther into her apartment. "I don't want to speak."

"Huh? So you're saying you not going to tell me what the hell happened to your face? Was it somebody I know?"

"I no talk, no," Jalissa said in almost a whisper and then her voice elevated into a loud shriek and said, "She no trust, Marisol. She no like me ask for Ryan."

Jason's heart sank. Her sister had whipped her ass because she kept asking where Ryan lived, because he kept pressuring her. He finally realized he was putting her in a precarious situation. If Ryan found out about them, he'd kill her. And from the look of her face, if her sister found out, then she'd put in work too.

Jason was overwhelmed with guilt. Ever since his crib got robbed by some unknown Hispanic men, he didn't know who to trust. He did have thoughts of letting Jalissa hold some money in a safety deposit box, but he changed his mind. He thought it better to have his moms open up a safe deposit box for him. That way, he'd be in control. He could spoon Cartier and Jalissa an allowance and have both women on a short leash.

Now, after Jalissa received this beat-down, he needed to rethink leaving her without any security. She had proven tonight that she loved him. As they say, a picture is worth a thousand words. The snapshot of her face read like a love story of her loyalty and devotion to him.

CHAPTER 14

Bossy

Cartier, Bam, and Li'l Momma decided to drive up to Sammy's in City Island to get some seafood on the warm, early summer day. It was three o'clock on a lazy afternoon when the ladies took the time together to plot their next move. With Cartier in the driver's seat, Bam and Li'l Momma sat back to enjoy the ride.

"So how much we got on the street?" Cartier asked no one in particular.

Li'l Momma spoke up. She was good with numbers. "Kenny got eighteen-five for us. He said we could pick it up anytime tomorrow. He's on his way back from Atlanta tonight. And Malik, Shawn, and Tiny all owe us forty large each. But that paper won't be ready for another week."

"Things are looking good," Cartier said. "I got an appointment with the realtor on Monday morning to show me some foreclosure properties. Y'all welcome to come if y'all bitches wanna get out of bed early enough to see where your money will be going."

"I trust you." Bam didn't want any parts of getting up early, nor sitting in any realtor's office.

"This isn't about trust, Bam. We're Cartel, so that should come without saying. The reason you and Li'l Momma should be there is because y'all might catch something I don't, and three sets of eyes are certainly better than one. I'm telling you, this real estate shit is gonna set us up for life. We're going to be millionaires the legal way. Once these investments pay off, no more hustling. Ever. I promise you that."

"I hear you, Cartier. Count me in. I'll be there," Li'l Momma said. "I wanna be the Donald Trump of the hood."

"Me too," Bam chimed in.

"Am I supposed to say, me three?" Cartier joked.

They all laughed.

Cartier pulled into the driveway, and as expected, it was packed. The parking lot was filled with high-end cars; Maseratis, Benz, Jaguars, BMWs, and Porsches. Cartier got out of Jason's Benz and had only taken a few steps before she was nearly run over by a black Porsche Cayenne. The music was blaring so loudly, the driver didn't hear Cartier's litany of curses, so she decided to wait. She was seething.

As the unsuspecting driver jumped out the driver's seat, he saw a shapely woman charging toward him. He adjusted his jeans, totally oblivious that the anger in her eyes were for his eyes only, and began to approach the restaurant.

"Where the fuck you get your license? The Internet? Didn't you see me standing here?"

Head looked around, not sure what was going on. "You talkin' to me?"

"Who the fuck you think I'm talking to? You coulda killed me!"

"Be easy, ma. I didn't see you." Head scanned the sexy Cartier up and down and liked what he saw, including the slick mouth all glossed up with lip gloss. "But then again, how could I miss someone as pretty as you?"

The compliment delayed Cartier's anger. She wasn't expecting the husky baritone voice and smooth dark chocolate skin.

"Why you driving all stupid like that anyway?" Cartier continued, not sure how to tone down her anger. "I mean, you act like you pushing a big-boy's toy."

Head couldn't help but laugh. Only weeks home from federal prison, he wasn't in any frame of mind to get into any dispute with anyone, especially a female.

"You sayin' I need to get my grown man on, huh?"

"You lookin' a little young in that Cayenne."

"I got grown-man money, though." He paused for emphasis. "My name is Head, by the way."

"Head? What type of name is Head?"

"Ask somebody, ma." Head walked into the restaurant.

Cartier didn't have to ask anyone. She knew he was a local legend, and she hated to admit it, but she was intrigued. BET's hit show, *American Gangster*, had profiled his life a few years back. People from his past were interviewed, including the arresting agents, their identities smudged out, detailing his rise and fall. The streets said he'd just got home, having done four years in a federal prison. He was given eighteen years to life, and on appeal his sentence was overturned, and ultimately he was acquitted, which when dealing with the feds, who everyone knows don't play fair, is unheard of.

The girls hustled into the restaurant as well, only to be told there was a forty-five-minute waiting list.

"You wanna wait at the bar?" Li'l Momma asked.

Cartier glanced over and saw that Head and his friend were already sitting down ordering drinks. He saw Cartier looking toward him and motioned for her to come over.

"Yo, that guy who nearly killed me is motioning for us to come over."

"He's a cutie, Cartier. What's his name?" Bam adjusted her clothes, hoping to catch the eye of the stranger.

"That's Head from Brownsville."

"Say word?" Li'l Momma said, her interest now piqued. "I heard of him."

"Haven't we all," Cartier remarked. "So, shall we go over?"

"Lead the way."

Li'l Momma and Bam followed Cartier over to the bar. Head stood up and pulled out the bar stool for Cartier, which immediately put a smile on her face.

Li'l Momma and Bam were thinking the same thing, both thinking they were the perfect candidates. *The moment he glances down and realizes she has a ring on her finger, he'll redirect his attention toward one of us.*

"What y'all ladies drinking?" Head asked.

Cartier turned toward her girls and mouthed the word *martinis*.

Bam and Li'l Momma both nodded their heads. "Apple martinis."

Head motioned for the bartender and ordered them their drinks. "This is my man, Clyde," he said.

"My name's Cartier, and this is Bam and Li'l Momma."

Head thought he'd heard those names before. He remembered hearing about a group of young girls who'd caught a body some years back. So many names were thrown around, but the one that stuck out in the *Daily News* was Cartier Timmons. Head thought he knew her mother.

"Yo, do one of y'all got a mother named Trina?"

Cartier grinned. "I do. How you know my mother?" Instantly she couldn't understand how pangs of jealousy shot through her. Did he sleep with her mother? He was at least forty years old.

"Your moms is mad cool. She used to fuck around with my man Nut back in the day. I'm talkin' way back in the late eighties, early nineties, some shit like that. Wow! It's a small world."

That's how Brooklyn was. If you put in work and made a name for yourself, it would last throughout the decades.

"Nut? Cartier, don't your husband know him?" Li'l Momma had already tossed down the apple martini and didn't like the way Clyde was leering at her. She'd already summed up that he was broke and that Head was the baller. If she locked him down, then she could see a bright future.

Cartier decided to ignore Li'l Momma.

Head glanced down at her ring.

"I cannot wait to tell Trina how you nearly killed her daughter."

"Nah, don't do that. Tell her I said whaddup. It would be good to see her. Why don't we exchange numbers, and you can call me when you're with her."

Everyone sitting there knew Head didn't give a fuck about no Trina. Bam and Li'l Momma sat on edge waiting to see Cartier's next move. Cartier could almost feel the energy being sucked out of the room.

"I'm in between cell phones right now, but give me your number, and I'll call you when I'm with Mom Duke."

Bam's and Li'l Momma's aspirations about pulling the legendary hustler went up in a mushroom cloud, but they were slightly happy that Cartier wouldn't be getting with him either. They both decided to make the best of the rest of the evening.

Head took charge and had the maître d' seat them at a table for five. There wasn't any way he was letting the spunky, convicted murderess out of his sight. He didn't give a fuck if she did have on ring on her finger.

❧

"So whatchu gonna do about Jason? You know if he find out, he gonna flip."

"And thank you for blowing me up in there," Cartier stated. "And find out what? That I got a telephone number for Trina? And what?"

"Don't bullshit me with that lame story. Just admit you checking for dude."

"I think *checking for* is too strong of a term. I mean, he's cute and funny."

"And dangerous. Don't forget, he got a rep. And you know you like a bad boy."

"Bitch, I'm married," Cartier joked.

"So? Jason ain't exactly the faithful husband." Bam had always had a deep-seated hatred toward Jason for pulling the trigger on Big Mike, and sometimes when the grief assassin crept in her dreams at night, making her relive the moment, the anger transferred to Cartier as well. But, so far, she was usually able to temper that and concentrate only on Jason.

Li'l Momma could never stand Bam's ability to ride Cartier's coattail. She was nothing but Cartier's cheerleader, if you let her tell it.

"Right now, you saying, because Jason cheats, Cartier should as well? If that's the case, then why get married? I know my marriage won't be like that."

Cartier wasn't in the mood. She hated that she and her friends found it hard to communicate without yelling and screaming, or taking shots at each other.

"I don't think it's realistic to say how your marriage will be, when you can't even keep a relationship," Carter retorted, "let alone get someone to take you seriously enough to marry you. And I know you're not dumb enough to think that a piece of paper will really keep a nigga faithful."

"I'm smart enough not to marry a hood nigga. I know that much. It's like they say: 'You get what you pay for.'"

"What's that supposed to mean?" Bam asked before Cartier could lose it on Li'l Momma.

"It means that there are plenty of corporate men out here that are marriage material. If I want a nigga to lace me with Gucci boots or keep my neck icy, I go to the local hustler. If I want a husband and father to my kids, I most certainly don't go to the local hustler. You feel me? Cartier set herself up for everything she's getting."

"I guess I could swallow that pill, if only hood niggas cheated. A cheater's a cheater, no matter what race or occupation. But until you are walking in my shoes"— Cartier cut her eyes at Li'l Momma—"then all you're doing is talking noise."

"Cartier, I'm not trying to get your pressure up."

"And you're not!"

"But I just think you deserve better. Since y'all hooked up, he's been publicly disrespecting you. I think you could do better. I mean, I know he blesses you with paper, but you can make your own paper. You had a rep way before y'all hooked up, and it's like he's taking your 'cool' points."

The more Cartier sat listening to Li'l Momma, the more her pressure rose. She wasn't angry with her friend for speaking the truth. Her anger began to fester and grow for her husband.

"I know you're probably thinking that I can't talk about this subject because I ain't married," Li'l Momma added, "but I feel there should be a level of respect. You can't even go to get your hair washed without wondering if the chick sitting across from you is on the down low with not just your baby daddy but your husband. Honestly, you're better than me, because there's no way I would have taken him back after he got my best friend pregnant. I could live a hundred years and will never swallow that bitter pill."

Bam was tired of listening to Li'l Momma preach. "Damn, Li'l Momma! Where's all of this coming from? You act like you're married to Jason. You know how these street niggas do. You've never really had a relationship where a dude wifed you, so you're really—"

"I know you didn't just say what I heard?" Li'l Momma swung her face around toward the backseat to face Bam. "And you have? Bam, please spare me. You had one dude who, while having a gun pointed at his head, made a remark that he was gonna make it official, and all of a sudden you're wifey material?"

"I know what we had!"

"What the fuck y'all have?" Li'l Momma said, getting hyped. "No, what you should have said is, you know what *he* had. He had a bullet put into his muthafuckin' brain, and you had an opportunity to spend his money, you low-down, grimy bitch!"

Bam burst into tears, unable to face the truth.

Cartier didn't even bother to referee the argument. She was still replaying her own issues in her marriage.

Li'l Momma continued, "That nigga wasn't ever gonna wife you. You were just a recreational fuck, hopping out of your bed two and three o'clock in the morning to go and get slayed. We call that a booty call on my side of town."

"At least I get booty calls, ho! Who the fuck ringing your phone?"

"Bam, please don't make me sling this pussy on one of your next beats, please. You know I keep a sponsor locked down, so fuck all that dumbness you talking."

"You're really feeling yourself for some strange reason," Bam yelled through tears. "But check this. Anyone that's checking for me will dodge your contaminated pussy, so you can sling your shit all you want. You won't be getting nowhere with the caliber of men I fuck with."

Li'l Momma erupted into an uncontrollable laughter.

Finally, Cartier had to ask, "What's so funny?"

"This chick is really slow. Like Donnie's beat-down really did make her a retard. Bam, I wouldn't crush you like this, but you asked for it. I already fucked one of your beats. Big Mike, sweetie. I slung, and he"—Li'l Momma popped her collar—"played catch!"

The news hit Bam and Cartier like a Mack truck. Only, Bam reacted. As she reached in her handbag to grab her gat, Li'l Momma peeped her reaching for something out of her peripheral vision. Swiftly, Li'l Momma unclasped her seatbelt and lunged toward the backseat, and both girls began tussling as Cartier continued to drive. Fists were flying everywhere, some landing on top of Cartier's head.

"Y'all better stop before we get killed!" Cartier screamed as she tried to find a safe place to park. She couldn't see out of any of her mirrors, and the sharp kicks into the back of her chair weren't helping things any. Next, she felt a clump of her hair being pulled, "Owwww!" Cartier screamed as the car jerked and headed dangerously into another lane. "Let go of my fucking hair!"

Bam had Cartier's hair, accidentally, but refused to let go. They were fighting to the finish. It seemed as if Cartier would never get the car to safety, but she did. Immediately, she hopped out and opened the back door, and Bam came tumbling out onto the hot pavement.

Cartier reached for Bam's bag and held it snugly, quickly moving out of the way as the two women ravaged each other. Cartier was somewhat amused, watching the two go at it. After the harsh transference of words, she knew they needed to get it out of their system.

"You tried to pull out on me?" Li'l Momma kept yelling as she continued to hit Bam with a flurry of blows.

Bam had handled herself well, but in the end, Li'l Momma got the better of her. When they both tired out, Li'l Momma turned to see Cartier perched on the side of the car.

"Why you didn't jump in and help ya girl?" Li'l Momma said, making light of the situation.

"I was waiting for the cops to roll up and take y'all to jail." Cartier shook her head. "We all need to go to anger management."

Both girls began to chuckle.

"Come on, let's get out of here." Cartier hopped back in the front seat to take everyone home.

Bam blurted out, "Fuck y'all bitches! Cartier, give me my bag!"

"Bam, come on and get in the car. It's over. Let me take you home."

"I said, give me my bag!"

Cartier looked up to see fresh purple bruises beginning to form on Bam's milk-chocolate skin. Her eyes were wild and shifty. Cartier opened up her bag, removed the gun and placed it on her lap, and then tossed Bam's bag out of the window. It hit the pavement like a bag of potatoes.

"Come on, Li'l Momma, let's bounce."

Once they drove off, Cartier turned to Li'l Momma. "Now why did you torture that girl like that? You know you didn't fuck no Big Mike."

"Of course, I didn't. Since when we get down like that? But if her psycho self was silly enough to believe it, then so be it."

"But, damn, what made you go there? You know Big Mike is a touchy subject."

"I don't care. She was taking shots at me, making me feel like I was a third-class citizen, that you and her belonged to some exclusive wifey club."

"Well, later I think you should call her and apologize, and I'll do the same. You know it's been rough on her."

Li'l Momma was silent for a while. "How long are we supposed to kiss her butt?"

"I guess, as long as it takes. And, really, I don't think you should be the one kissing her butt. That should come from me. But I do think you could rein in your temper somewhat, just for the sake of peace. And, believe me, I know how hard that could be. Bam has a way off getting under anyone's skin, and before you know it, you've already snapped."

"You know what?" Li'l Momma turned to face Cartier. "What do you think she would have done, had I not stopped her from getting into her purse?"

Both ladies didn't want to speculate.

"I think, when you call her, you should ask her."

The sharp pain in her side was an indication of what was to come. Cartier tried to turn over and sleep through the pain, but it was too intense. She didn't even have enough time to get angry about waking up to an empty bed. Jason had spent yet another night out. Almost crawling to the bathroom, she was eager to relieve her full bladder, until her urine came flowing out like fire.

"Oouucchhh!" she screamed, her eyes welling up with tears. "That muthafucka!"

Cartier didn't need a doctor to know that Jason had given her an STD. She needed her girls, calling Bam and then Li'l Momma, and demanding, "Please, meet me at Trina's house in an hour!"

Any morsel of love she felt for Jason was dead. Finally she felt ready to implement the plan that had been swirling around in her head for weeks. She just needed to know that her girls would be down for whatever.

❧

Jalissa didn't know who burnt who, because Jason wasn't the only guy she was seeing. Nor did she know who the father of her unborn child was, for that same reason. But she did know how she would go about handling both those issues.

Screaming into the telephone, she let out a flurry of Spanish words, throwing in *disease* and then *pregnant*.

Jason knew he was busted. He'd already been to the clinic a week ago, so he knew that more than a few chicks would be calling to curse him out. Even his doctor gave him a tongue-lashing for having unprotected sex at his age. But Jason just didn't get the same feeling putting on a condom. For him, it was like getting in a hot tub with rubber boots on.

Jalissa's outburst was the least of his worries. She wasn't his wife. He knew Cartier would surely act violent, but so far, she hadn't said a word. Foolishly, he thought he hadn't contaminated her. The next issue was Jalissa's pregnancy.

"So what are you gonna do?"

"I no keep," she cried into the phone.

Jason was sure she would have wanted to keep his baby. Her response made him challenge her. "What do you mean, you're not going to keep my baby? I thought you were a good girl. You believe in abortion?"

"I no keep. I no want your wife to leave."

After everything he'd put her through, burning her and getting her pregnant, she still had the kindest heart to think of his situation with Cartier, sacrificing her own morals and happiness. Jason was certainly smitten with this one.

"Look, don't worry about my wife. You keeping my baby, and I don't want to hear you talk about no abortion."

"But it cost *mucho dinero* for baby."

"Jalissa!"

"Yes, *papi*."

"Don't worry about that. I got you."

CHAPTER 15

Expiration Date

"**B**itch, you already know what this is. Don't say a word, and you won't get hurt."

"Yo, what the fuck you doing?" Jalissa asked, looking down at the barrel of the .45 pointed directly at her abdomen. Once she saw the seriousness in Cartier's expression, her *'I no speaka English'* act was dead.

The hard whack on the back of her head with the butt of the gun buckled her knees and instantly dazed her. Woozy and temporarily blinded, she was unable to think straight, as fear shot straight through her veins. Her hands trembled as she tried to massage the back of her head at the point of impact.

"Didn't I tell you not to say a muthafuckin' word?" Cartier's voice was stern as she growled instructions. "Now get the fuck in the car. Move!"

Fearfully, Jalissa crawled into the backseat of Jason's Benz, where once again Bam was at the driver's seat and Li'l Momma was riding shotgun. Cartier scooted in the back with the crying hostage to better control the situation.

"Don't cry now," Bam taunted. "Your ass should have known better than to fuck with The Cartel."

"Remember me, bitch?" Li'l Momma's icy glare cut through Jalissa's heart. "You was all up in my grill a few months ago, and all the time you knew Ryan killed our friends. You slimy bitch!"

As Carter's friends mocked Jalissa, Cartier remained quiet, readying her mind for what would come next. At this point the outcome hung in Jason's hands; except, he didn't know it.

Bam drove to the motel where Cartier had a crackhead rent a room only hours earlier. Cartier dragged Jalissa out and instructed Bam to park across the street in the KFC parking lot and try to remain out of sight.

"When I'm done here, I'll come to you. But keep your eyes open for anything that could go wrong. Anything suspicious, y'all better come in there blazing."

"Well, what about her? You can handle her by yourself? You want me to come in with you?" Li'l Momma asked, because her friend was obviously not telling them the whole story.

"Can I handle her?" Cartier asked, a smirk plastered on her face, before walking away and dragging Jalissa with her.

As soon as the motel room slammed shut, Cartier tucked her gun inside her waist and commenced to whipping Jalissa's ass, her Brooklyn trademark Timberland boot smashing repeatedly into Jalissa's fragile body parts.

"Keep fighting back!" Cartier taunted, as Jalissa threw feeble punches that couldn't do damage to a ten-year-old.

She was no match for the angry, betrayed, skillful fighter. "That's right. You think you're a tough bitch, right? You and your sister, huh, bitch!"

With the uppercuts to the chin and gut, headlocks, and barrage of punches to her face and head, the pain was so unbearable, Jalissa was ready to close her eyes and accept death.

When Cartier's arms finally got tired, and Jalissa stopped putting up a fight, she was duct-taped and propped in a cheap, flimsy chair to await her fate.

At that point, Cartier called Jason. "Where you at?"

"I'm laying on that nigga Ryan, but he ain't coming through."

"Ryan? You got a locale on him?"

"Didn't you just hear me say he ain't coming through?" Jason replied, agitated.

Cartier tossed her eyes in the air. "Yo, meet me at Surfside Motel right before you drive through Far Rockaway. I got the 4-1-1 on Ryan, and my information is the real deal. So you better get over here, not now but *right* now!"

Cartier wiped down the motel room before walking casually across the boulevard to where Bam and Li'l Momma were waiting. She eased into the backseat. "Drive!"

Bam hesitated. "What happened in there? We saw Jason pull up. You left him in there with Jalissa?"

Cartier collapsed into tears. "I'm not going to say it again. Now drive!"

The tone in her voice was filled with angst. Bam panicked and sped out of the parking lot, tires screeching, doing nearly eighty miles an hour.

Li'l Momma screamed, "Bam, slow down! You know we're in here riding dirty. You want us all to go to jail?"

"I'm just trying to get away—"

"From what? Cartier ain't even told us what happened. You trying to outrun an affair? 'Cause, right now, that's all that could happen, leaving Jason and his mistress alone."

For some reason Li'l Momma's sarcasm made everyone in the vehicle erupt in laughter. Even the miserable, quite shaken up Cartier let out a hearty laugh.

When they reached Bam's house, Cartier had composed herself enough to tell her friends, "Bam was right for jetting. We just left the scene of a double homicide."

CHAPTER 16

Dead Men Tell No Tales

"Ma, Jason's not coming home."

"What? He got knocked?" Trina sat up in her bed, still woozy from hanging out the previous night at Club Rendezvous, in the heart of Bedford-Stuyvesant, Brooklyn.

"Nah, he ain't get knocked," Cartier said sternly, trying not to let her emotions get the better of her. "He got himself murdered."

Trina didn't know how to handle the news. Sure, it was a risk and always the highest possibility each time Jason walked out the front door, but Trina was in denial.

"Oh, Cartier, baby, I'm so sorry," Trina began. Visions of the children growing up without a father flashed before her. What were they going to do now that the breadwinner was gone? How long would Cartier hold down the monthly expenses? Cartier would have to go back out there and do what she knew how to do best.

Straightaway Trina's eyes began to well up with tears. Then she looked at her daughter, who was emotionless. Surely she was in shock.

"Cartier, come in here and sit down. Tell me what happened. Who called you? Are they sure it was Jason? Did you try to call him? Do you think that Spanish bitch set him up?"

Cartier swallowed hard. "I gave him a chance to come clean, to make a choice, and he chose her, so I had to do what I had to do."

Trina looked into her daughter's eyes. She didn't see despair, hurt, pain, confusion, or shock, but anger, betrayal, and a coldness she knew too well.

"Cartier, what did you do?"

"Ma, I can't believe it either. I mean, I knew I could do it, but I didn't know I would do it."

"Tell me what you did!" Trina yelled, tired of the cat-and-mouse game her daughter dragged her into. "Did you kill Jason?"

"Yes."

"What! Why, Cartier?"

"It's like I told you, I didn't have a choice."

"Are you fuckin' crazy? Do you think I want to lose you again to prison? Only, this time you'll get life, Cartier. You hear me? Life!"

Cartier couldn't believe Trina was flipping out. Usually she was down for whatever. "Why are you yelling at me?"

"I should slap the black off you! Did you ever stop to think about Cee Cee or Jason Jr. growing up without a father?"

"Well it's not like I can click my heels three times and go back to Kansas," Cartier remarked, dryly.

"Sometimes I wonder about you, Cartier. You can be chilly as an iceberg, and I know you don't get that from me." Trina's voice was laced with disappointment.

Cartier knew, if she needed anyone on her side, it would have to be Trina. Her mother was her rock. The only person she could run to when things got rough.

"So you'd rather me be dead?"

"What are you talking about? Of course, I wouldn't rather it be you." Trina reached for her Newport and lit one up. "Stop talking in riddles 'cause you working my last nerve, chile."

"Jason and Jalissa were secretly building a life together. We already knew that he took all of our money—"

"Yeah. So? That doesn't mean he was gonna take you out of this world."

"What the fuck! When did you become his cheerleader?"

"This is wrong!"

"Well, since you know so much, know this. Know that Jason got Jalissa pregnant, and Jason told her that he'd stand by and let Ryan get at me and he wouldn't do shit! He was gonna let Ryan kill me, just as he did Monya and Shanine! Now do you still want to take up for your son-in-law? I thought you were the mother who said she didn't want to go through what Janet went through."

Cartier didn't tell the true story. She couldn't admit to Trina that her jealous rage killed Jason. That her husband had cheated on her for the last time. He'd put another chick before her one too many times, and at that point something in Cartier had snapped and there was no turning back.

And truthfully, as she sat there, she wasn't sure she'd even want to go back and take back what she'd done. All she kept seeing was how hurt Jason looked when he walked through the door and saw the badly beaten Jalissa. And how he kept trying to get her to leave so he could save his ho.

To Trina, this new news was startling, yet believable. Jason was doing foul shit all the time. "How did you find all this out?"

"You know Bam is a wealth of information. We should call her Perez Hilton 'cause she stay getting the scoop." Cartier's attempted joke fell flat in the midst of all the tension. "Anyway, Bam got word that Jason and Jalissa were plotting against me and when I confronted him, he didn't deny it." Cartier hoped that Trina's line of questioning would soon stop, or else she would get caught up in her lies.

"Oh, so you confronted his slick ass?" Trina's pressure began to go up with thoughts of laying Cartier to rest. She just couldn't bear that.

"Yeah, Ma, and you should have saw the cocky look on his face. Like I said, he made his choice. I pulled out and let off a dozen shots into not only him but his bitch too."

Trina smiled. "Oh, you got that ho too?"

"Sure did."

"Cartier, please tell me that no one saw you and that

you did your dirt by yourself. I don't want another situation with The Cartel flipping on you."

"I'm good. I handled my business alone, but I think we should turn on the news to see if in fact it's relevant enough to make the news."

Cartier's admission wasn't totally false. No one was there to actually see the murders, but Bam and Li'l Momma were involved and could easily be charged as accessories after the fact.

It took about thirty minutes before they found the story on the news. As the reporter stood in front of the motel and ran down the details of the night's incident, Trina and Cartier's mouths both dropped.

CHAPTER 17

Lies and Alibis

"Mrs. Payne?"

"Yes."

"Ma'am, there's been a terrible incident last night. Your husband was shot and is in critical condition at Brookdale Hospital. I think you should get here as quickly as possible. He underwent eight hours of surgery, and things aren't looking too good. I think you should gather all your family and bring them to say their good-byes. I'm sorry to be the one to tell you this information."

So it was true. Jason didn't die on the dingy motel room floor with Jalissa. Last night the news reported that there had been a murder and an attempted murder at the Surfside Motel. The reporter went on to say that the female victim was DOA and the male victim had been rushed to Brookdale in critical condition, barely clinging on to his life.

At this point Cartier was freaking out. How in heaven's name could he have survived taking all those bullets? Cartier was almost positive her aim was spot-on. She hated to face reality, but if Jason made a full recovery there wouldn't be any "let's kiss and make up." It's not like she could just say sorry and let bygones be bygones. She had killed his mistress and unborn child and tried to kill him. What could she do to make things back right? Put him on a guilt trip and tell him that he made her do it and plead temporary insanity? She was sure the first moment Jason opened his eyes, he'd want those same eyes to see Cartier in a pine box.

The putrid hospital odor assaulted Cartier's nose as she traveled through the main level of the hospital up to the Intensive Care Unit, where the head surgeon was awaiting her arrival. The petite, well-spoken Indian woman greeted Cartier with a warm smile. Her eyes displayed her fatigue from nearly going twenty hours without sleep.

"Mrs. Payne?"

"Yes. Hello, Doctor Kumar."

"We worked really hard on your husband, and I'm delighted to say he's a fighter. He's a strong man, Mrs. Payne. Most people in his condition would have expired. He has something to live for."

"So, he's going to pull through?" Cartier tried to sound hopeful, to not sound disappointed. "He'll make a full recovery?"

"Yes, he's expected to make a full recovery, but it will take a while. He'll heal at his own pace, and he'll need to work with a physical therapist once he regains his strength back. You'll need to be strong for him because he'll need you to help him bounce back from such a traumatic experience."

Physical therapy, Cartier thought. Perhaps she didn't have anything to fear with Jason so fucked up from taking all those bullets.

"When you say he'll need physical therapy, like, what are we talking about? Does he have control over his bowel movement? Is he a vegetable? Can he walk? Hold a gu— can he grip things?"

"Right now it's hard to say. But, as I said, he'll need extensive physical therapy, and it could take months, maybe even years for him to make a full recovery. This'll be hard on you and your family. There's counseling available for everyone, but let's just take this one day at a time. Right now, thank God that he even pulled through. One bullet lodged two-tenths of a centimeter from his heart."

"Thank you, Doctor Kumar. Can I see him now?"

"Now isn't a good time. He needs his rest. Give him at least eight hours before you come to see him. Besides, he's fully sedated." Doctor Kumar cleared her throated and then gave Cartier a sympathetic pat on her shoulder for reassurance. "Don't worry, your husband will be fine. But before you go, a few detectives would like to speak with you."

"With me?"

"Yes, it's just a routine for any gunshot wounds. They'll most likely ask you if your husband had any enemies, things like that. Come with me. I'll escort you to the vestibule." Doctor Kumar paused and looked deeply into Cartier's eye. "Mrs. Payne?"

"Yes?"

"Are you all right? I know this is a lot for such a young woman, but believe me, your husband is a fighter, and he's in good hands."

The doctor tried to comfort Cartier with her words and tone. She did read fear in her eyes, but it wasn't for her husband's death. She feared that he lived.

❧

"Ma'am, my name is Detective O'Leary, and this is my partner, Detective Graves."

Both detectives were women, which threw Cartier slightly off her game face. Women were suspicious by nature, so Cartier knew she had to be as blunt as possible to fuck their heads up.

"First, let me start off by saying, it's unfortunate, what happened to your husband, but did you—"

"Do you know who was the bitch he was fucking?"

"Excuse me?"

"The news said that there was a woman found murdered in the motel room with my husband. Who was she?"

"Well, we were going to ask you exactly that."

Of course, you were, Cartier thought. *You were going to try to establish a motive.* "You asking the wrong person. Try coming back here tomorrow and ask that slimy bastard who the fuck he was shacking up with!"

"You don't seem too concerned that your husband got filled with bullets. Can I ask where you were last night around nine p.m.?"

"I was home with my kids."

"How old are your children?"

"Four years old."

"Not old enough to vouch for your alibi."

"I don't need an alibi, but if I did, my mother was there too. And, as I said, if you want to know what happened to Jason, come back tomorrow and stop wasting my time. I'm a jilted wife at the moment whose husband just got shot up, fucking some skank bitch, so excuse me, and give me some time to wallow in my misery."

"Why are you so sure that Jason will even wake up tomorrow or anytime soon?"

"Because he promised me he would never leave me out here to raise our kids alone, that's how." With that line, Cartier could see she had one of the detectives eating out the palm of her hands.

The other one wasn't that easy. "Did you know your husband was having an affair?"

"Yes, I did. Did I know with who? No. I would have beat the brakes off of her and then fucked him up too."

"Perhaps even killed him?"

"As you can see, my husband ain't dead. If you'll excuse me . . . I have two kids at home who need their mother." Cartier's heart felt like it was about to rip through her chest, but she managed to put up a good front. She turned on her heel and left the two detectives standing in front of Jason's room, stuck on stupid.

Once the elevator doors closed, Cartier finally exhaled, wiping sweat from her brow as she rode to the ground level.

As she exited the elevator, something pulled her gaze across the room. She and Marisol locked eyes. Marisol was coming from out the back of the hospital, where she had come to ID her sister's body. The beauty was stoic as she walked out of the coroner's room, head held high, hair pulled tightly back, revenge plastered on her face.

At that moment Cartier knew the beef with her husband and mistress didn't end on the filthy motel room floor as she'd thought; it had just begun.

CHAPTER 18

It Ain't Over Till It's Over

Each day for six days Cartier went to check up on Jason's status in the hospital. Cartier knew two things were certain: She'd have to face Jason again, and he would surely seek revenge. One small part of her heart kept telling her that she could explain away her actions. Put him on a guilt trip and let bygones be bygones.

Perhaps they could just divorce and continue to raise their kids as supportive parents. In her heart, she knew it was hard pulling that trigger, but in her mind she would do it again, if he forced her hand.

When Doctor Kumar had called to tell her that Jason was no longer going in and out of consciousness, that he'd requested to see her, she exhaled.

"You gotta finish what you started," Trina said when she saw the spooked look on her daughter's face. "Go there and see where his head is at. For all you know, he could snitch you out to five-o."

"Ma, Jason would never go out like that. He's a thorough dude. You know that. He would never talk to those peoples. Under any circumstance. How pussy would he look, snitching out his wife? He'd never live that down out on these streets. You feel me?"

"Well, if you done shot all the fight out of him, he might not have a choice but to use the police for reinforcement."

"If he felt like things were looking grim, and physically he'd never be able to seek revenge, then Wonderful would inherit his beef, and he would be the one to take out next." Cartier shook her head. "Don't think that I haven't thought about what would happen if Jason went to the police. But something inside my gut keeps telling me that even if physically he wasn't up to getting at me, snitching would never be an option. Sure, some people do snitch, but not all people would snitch. And let's not forget when five-o snatched him up for suspicion of murdering Donnie. Even though he was looking as guilty as anyone, he held his tongue. Ma, I just gotta believe he'll keep it street."

Cartier rolled up to the hospital in Jason's luxury vehicle and found a park right outside. She'd taken to wearing form-fitting dresses and stilettos, with her .25 strapped to her inner thigh. It was a cunningly deceiving look that made her look vulnerable.

As she exited the elevator on the third floor, two stationed police officers were at their post, as requested by the chief of police. Moments later, the two detectives working the case came out with looks of frustration.

"I guess Doctor Kumar called y'all as well," Cartier casually remarked. "Is he talking?"

"He's talking, but he ain't saying anything credible. Perhaps you'll have a better chance at getting him to finger who killed an innocent woman and tried to kill him, because the story he's telling ain't ringing true."

"So I'm going from suspect to snitch?"

"Excuse me?"

"You heard me. First, you accuse me of murdering some wannabe wifey and filling my husband with holes. Now you're coming to me for my help and asking me to elicit information from my husband and run and tell you? Get the fuck outta here!" Cartier was truly feeling herself, relieved that Jason hadn't sold her out.

The lanky Detective Graves, nostrils flaring, stepped just a few inches from Cartier's face. Cartier could smell her dragon breath.

"If you interfere with our investigation, I'll have your ass thrown back in the slammer faster than your hoodlum husband will recuperate. You think you tough shit 'cause you did a murder bid? That shit don't scare me!"

Just as Cartier thought. They did know about her past, which meant she was under investigation while Jason was in a coma.

"And your badge don't scare me. If you didn't have it on, I'd wear your ass out. Now get the fuck outta my face with your threats. I'm a grieving wife getting harassed by the police, and if you keep it up, I'll have the news plastered in front of the police precinct with picket signs and the whole nine. You don't know who I know. I'll have Al Sharpton in my corner, so fuck around if you want to."

For a few intense seconds the ladies participated in a stare-down, until Detective O'Leary pulled her partner away.

Cartier spun on her heels, rolled her eyes at the two remaining police guards, and then walked in to see Jason.

I really fucked him up. Cartier looked at all the tubes hanging out. Two intravenous tubes dripped pain medication to help ease his suffering. The endotracheal tube that was helping him breathe was now removed for a tracheotomy, a voice box to help him speak, and there was a large metal wire cast with wire transplants to hold the position and set his left arm, which one of the bullets had lodged into and broken dozens of bones.

As Cartier approached the bed, Jason eyed her. He didn't have to say a word. His silence spoke volumes. She returned his glare with the same contempt. She swallowed any empathy she had for him. Not only did she warn him that she wasn't going to take any more of his disrespectful behavior, but there was still over a million dollars out of her reach—money he'd taken to set up him and his new bitch in their new life.

Thoughts of little Christian living in a roach motel while Jason prepared to have his little half-Puerto Rican love child made Cartier feel justified. Jason needed to charge it to the game. He'd gambled on Jalissa, and now he knew she was no match for Cartier.

"Was she worth it?" Cartier mocked. "As you lie here all fucked up, do you still think about her white skin and soft hair?"

Cartier still couldn't contain her jealousy, even with Jalissa buried and gone. As images of them making love flashed before her eyes, she leaned over and whispered, "How does it feel to know that I took your seed from you? Your child gasping for air as the life drained from Jalissa? A child you'll never be able to hold?" She stood up.

A single tear slid down Jason's face. Finally he spoke. It sounded like auto-tune. "It . . . ain't . . . over . . . until . . . I . . . say . . . it's . . . over."

Cartier plopped down on the side of his hospital bed, crossed her legs, and seductively hoisted up her skirt, slightly revealing her .25. "The day you walk out of here is the day I finish what I started. If I were you, I'd take my time recovering."

CHAPTER 19

99 Problems

As spring arrived, Cartier started to relax again. She'd been on edge for months, always alert and looking over her shoulders. Jason must have heeded her warning because he was certainly taking his time recuperating. The hospital had moved him to a rehabilitation center in upstate New York, from where a nurse called weekly to update the family on his progress.

In the meantime, Ryan and Marisol had somewhat dropped from the face of the earth. Cartier's Cartel couldn't get an address, vehicle description, local hangout, nothing on the two. Cartier even kept on Wonderful and Blake, who thought Ryan was behind Jason's attempted murder, which Cartier used to her advantage. She kept drilling into their heads, "Until Ryan is dead, the beef still lives on."

Meanwhile, business was booming for The Cartel. Together they'd purchased a six-story tenement building on Parkside Avenue near Prospect Park with large rooms, 54 apartments (all occupied), and a superintendent already living onsite under a foreclosure. The original owner had bought the property back in 1972 for $190,000, which was top dollar back then. The property had appreciated at one time to close to $4.0 million. During the '80s, at the height of the crack epidemic, the building had become dilapidated. The City of New York stepped in and began fining those slum lords, and by 1994 the landlord had made all the necessary repairs. Now he was tired and weary, and the real estate and stock market had sucked him dry for the fortune he'd amassed throughout the years. One by one, the bank began seizing his properties.

That's where Cartier came in. There were several prospective buyers for the listing, priced at $575,000. Cartier's Cartel offered him an all-cash deal of $450,000 and closed within ten days. She knew that in fifteen years or so the market would turn back around and their investment would be worth over ten million, with its close proximity to the park. In real estate it was all about location. The neighborhood was under major revitalization, and although she was black and proud, as an investor she was more than pleased that the building's demographic consisted of mostly Caucasians, who were ultimately taking over the neighborhood.

Her mother had told her that, in the late '80s, Flatbush consisted mostly of West Indians, thus the famous West Indian Day parade. Now, not only was it mostly Orthodox Jewish families, but also white yuppies catching the D train on their way into the city to make a boatload of cash.

To keep things professional and also to have their taxes prepared properly, Cartier hired an outside building management company to collect the rent each month, handle evictions if need be, and send all the proper documents to their accountant. Cartier didn't want to be just a drug dealer. She wanted to make smart investments with the illegal money and become a respected businesswoman; someone her kids could look up to. While she was incarcerated, she'd read stories about the John D. Rockefeller, Joseph Kennedy, and William R. Heart, where it was rumored that the foundation of their money came from prohibition, mob ties, prostitution, extortion, the whole gamut. And instead of ending up in jail, they all had their names cemented in our history books as moguls.

As the Mercedes' Michelin tires glided down the Belt Parkway, Cartier kept hitting replay on Jay-Z's and Alicia Keys' New York anthem. The song made Cartier feel unstoppable. No matter how much she'd ever thought of leaving her hometown, she couldn't help but feel grateful to be born and raised in New York. And it's true what they say: "If you can make it in New York, you can make it anywhere."

Cartier arrived at Bam's apartment, and instead of calling her to come down, she needed to go inside to pee. As soon as she got off the elevator, the aroma nearly sucked the clean air out of her lungs. She inched closer to Bam's door and smelled the familiar odor.

"I don't believe this shit," Cartier said out loud. She banged aggressively on the front door.

"Hold the fuck up!" Bam returned, not knowing or caring who was at the front door. Seconds later, a lazy-eyed Bam opened the door with a huge Kool-Aid type grin plastered on her silly face.

Cartier pushed past her and went straight to the living room where there was an ashtray with something burning. "What's that you smoking?"

"A blunt."

"I know it's a fucking blunt! What I look like? What the fuck is inside it?"

"Damn, Cartier. Could you stop yelling! I'm not your child. Go and chastise your kids because I'm really not in the mood for any bullshit today."

Bam's feistiness had somewhat annoyed Cartier, but deep down inside, she knew Bam was right. Most times Cartier did treat them like she was their mother, but in her eyes it came with the territory. She was the head of the crew, and she actually enjoyed controlling their every movement.

The other members should understand that she came off bossy because she was the boss. Single-handedly she had guided them up through the food chain to a place where they could afford their own whips, jewelry, clothes, and now real estate. She put each one of them in a position where they didn't need no man for the "college plan." The $54.11 Reebok was never an option.

Cartier could see Bam was toasted and decided to take it down a notch.

"I'm not trying to start nothing. I'm just asking what's in the blunt, because it's permeating the whole floor. You're lucky that I'm knocking and not po-po."

Bam exhaled and began combing her hair in the mirror. "It's just a little Acapulco gold weed and a thin line of bomb."

"Bomb?"

"Coke, Cartier, damn."

"Since when you start smoking crack?"

"Crack?"

"This shit is crazy. What's going on with you? We don't use our product! That's against the code of the streets."

"So now I'm a crackhead?" Bam broke out into a maniacal laughter that only crazy people have mastered.

Cartier was taken aback by her strange behavior. Finally she replied, "You tell me."

"Hell, muthafuckin', no!" Bam was insulted once she realized Cartier was serious.

"Well, that's what it could lead to."

Bam tossed the comb on the sofa and faced Cartier. "Look, drop it. It's just a recreational get-high to cope with the fact that I participated in getting the love of my life murdered, and it helps me to sleep at night without seeing his brains splattered all over his living room."

"Bam, stop bringing up Big Mike! Especially now that you're using. You say that shit in front of the wrong person, and we're all going to jail."

"Stop bringing it up? As if it's that easy! This shit is fucking me up."

"So get a religion, ask for forgiveness, something, but I don't want to hear his name again. Nothing will bring him back. Nothing will make it better. Now, if it's any consolation to you, you and I are in the same boat. Look what I had to do to Jason. He was the love of my life too. But before men we're The Cartel, and they both were connected in some way to what happened to Shanine and Monya. And let's not forget that when you found out Jason was fucking with Jalissa, you specifically told me that Jason couldn't get a pass. And he didn't. I did that for you. Because I love you, and we fam."

"Cartier, don't tell me that bullshit, you did it for me. You did it for YOU! Your jealousy tried to kill Jason. That shit ain't have nothing to do with me, Shanine, and damn sure, not Monya, because what you really did was almost leave Monya's child without a father. And, for the record, I'm not some dumb-ass, drugged-out junkie who can't hold her tongue. Because of you, Donnie beat my brains out, and I never sold us out. It was your little *girlfriend* who cracked under the pressure, so spare me the *I'm-the-weakest-link* lecture. I got more heart than you give me credit for!"

Cartier no longer wanted to go back and forth. Bam was clearly high. "Bam, we could go tit for tat all morning. I didn't come here for this. I thought we were going to buy you and Li'l Momma some whips."

Bam stared at Cartier with contempt but quickly let it go.

❦

Truth be told, Bam didn't want anyone to know she'd started tapping her blunts with cocaine. It all happened accidentally. Lately she'd been hanging out a lot, trying to get her mind past what had happened with Big Mike. She went to a grimy basement party in Brooklyn and ended up having the time of her life. It was a BYOB type of atmosphere, so Bam brought a bottle of Henny and within two hours had downed almost a whole liter herself. The last thing she remembered was some cutie telling her she was acting sloppy drunk and needed to mellow out.

He passed her what she thought was only weed, and the first pull from the blunt had Bam flying high. The impact from the long drag off the blunt stopped her heart momentarily until she got used to the potent drug. The next morning, she woke up naked next to the stranger—obviously, they'd fucked—with a massive hangover. As she prepared to leave, she asked if he had a blunt for her to take for the road.

"Twenty-five dollars," he said.

"What? For a blunt? Damn, nigga, if you wanna play it like that I should be charging you for last night, and I promise you it'll be more than twenty-five dollars."

"Ma, first off, I remember last night, and you weren't that good. And this ain't just a blunt. It's Acapulco gold weed laced with pure white Colombian coke."

Bam was shell-shocked. "Did you just say you gave me coke to smoke? Like I'm some fuckin' trick!" Bam's voice had risen to a high-pitched scream.

"Yo, calm down with all that bullshit and take the bass out of your voice before I have to handle your stupid ass in here. Matter fact"—The stranger jumped to his feet. He stood over six feet tall, and was posturing, to intimidate Bam—"it's time for you to get the fuck out. Now I'm asking your dumb ass politely. The next time I have to ask, my fist won't be so nice."

"Bitch, if you so much as raise your hand to me, I'll see you dead! You must not know who the fuck I am. My name is Bam. Head bitch of The Cartel. My crew and I rock niggas like you to sleep every day, so I suggest you check my resume, and you'll find out that the last two niggas who went up against us are DEAD. So I suggest your bum ass—"

"I don't give a fuck who you repping! I will—"

Bam was quick with her .45, which she steadied directly at his head.

His eyes flew open in horror. He couldn't believe she'd actually pulled out on him. Perhaps there was some truth to what the Brooklynite was saying. "Chill, ma. That coke got you all jumpy and shit. It ain't that serious. We had a good time last night. Let's not ruin it with all these theatrics, 'cause a dude like me isn't for all that drama. You feel me?"

Bam felt empowered as she stood there, cocky, pointing her pistol at the cowardly cokehead. *Was this all it took?* she thought. *A gun and the heart to use it? Could that be the key from going from Indian to Chief?*

Bam didn't want to understand why she'd lied about being the head of The Cartel. All she knew was, she felt good saying it.

After Cartier scooped up Bam, they headed to pick up Li'l Momma. Both ladies were going to the used car lot on Northern Boulevard in Queens to buy them some much-needed whips. They'd grown tired of hopping in cabs or waiting for Cartier to come and pick them up. And since business was booming and Jason was out of the picture for the moment, they all decided they needed a distraction.

"So tell us again why we have to buy used?" Li'l Momma asked.

"You don't *have* to do shit. But if you were smart, you'd buy used because, for one thing, vehicles are overpriced. The moment you drive off the lot, your car has already depreciated in value, unlike real estate, where property value, if you hold it long enough, will appreciate. And, secondly, these used dealers are the shadiest characters. We can walk in there and drop forty, fifty grand on the table, and they won't report it to the IRS. Ten thousand dollars or over in cash has to be reported, and guess what, genius? You ain't ever worked a day in your life. And the most important thing is that you won't have a car note. If shit gets fucked up, you won't have the repo man coming in the middle of the night, towing your shit away with your Gucci bag and Louboutin's in the trunk. So, Li'l Momma, ain't nobody twisting your arm here. You can easily walk your ass into any dealer you want. I could give less than a fuck."

"I see somebody woke up on the wrong side of the bed. All I did was ask a freaking question."

"A question I already answered."

Li'l Momma took her finger and drew an imaginary circle around her face. "Stupid girl." Then she took the same finger and circled Cartier. "Smart girl." She then rolled her eyes to hammer home that she got the point.

Bam knew Cartier was on edge from catching her smoking the coke. Which Bam felt was Cartier's own fault for coming early. Still, she didn't want tension on what was supposed to be a fun day out with the girls, so she decided to stroke Cartier's ego.

"Yo, Cartier, I'm not trying to be sarcastic here, but you are a smart girl. Like how you know so much about all this shit? Real estate, car value, plots, business? Did you read books or something while being locked down?"

Cartier almost didn't want to answer such a stupid question.

"I listen. I keep my ears open and listen to other people's pitfalls. When you hear somebody say what they shoulda done, when you get the same chance, try doing the opposite of what they did, and do what they shoulda did. We ain't the first chicks to sell drugs, and we won't be the last. There's an art to staying ahead of the game, and I refuse for any of us to take the same old fall that most hustlers take. I want better not only for me, my kids, and Trina, but you two as well. We're all we got, and we're fam. Y'all are like my blood sisters, and I don't want to lose any one of you for something careless. Not only do we have to stay alert for the local drug rivals, but the beef that we still have with Ryan, and the feds and five-o are on the list as well."

"Speaking of Ryan, ain't nobody heard shit about his whereabouts?" Li'l Momma said.

"Not one word, which worries me somewhat. And what about his bitch?" Bam asked.

"Marisol?"

"Yeah, her. Do you think she knows that you murked her sister?"

"Don't know. Don't care."

"Well, maybe you should. You just said you didn't want us taking any chances, and to always watch our backs to avoid unnecessary pitfalls. I just feel that she could be a problem."

"So what are you saying?" Cartier asked Li'l Momma, although she already knew what was up.

"I'm saying that after we have our fun today, we got to get back to the business—street business—and tie up all loose ends. We need to get our hit list and start crossing off names, because I'll be damned if I'm going to be a walking target. Once all of this is said and done, then we can start focusing back on our legal businesses. But if we're dead, then that really wouldn't make any sense now, would it?"

CHAPTER 20

The Chase

The incessant ringing of Cartier's cell phone irked her nerves. It was barely seven o'clock in the morning, and she was having a luxurious sleep, dreaming about Lotto numbers and red velvet cake. Ignoring the caller wasn't enough. They were unstoppable. Finally she gave in and growled, "Hello!" in a hoarse, impatient tone.

"Good morning. Is this Cartier?"

The voice was unfamiliar, so Cartier pulled the phone from her ear to look at the telephone number, which was unrecognizable. She exhaled. "Who's this?"

"This is Head. Are you 'sleep?"

Immediately Cartier sat straight up in bed and tried to adjust her voice. "No, no, I'm not 'sleep. But how did you get my number?"

He laughed. "Meet me at Lindenwood Diner in an hour for breakfast, and I'll tell you what you wanna know."

Cartier panicked. "What are—"

"Don't be late. I'm not the most patient person."

"Maaaaa!" Cartier screamed and ran downstairs like a crazy person into her mother's bedroom, startling Trina.

"What's wrong?" Trina asked. "God, please tell me that nothing else has happened."

"Nah, ain't shit bad happen." Cartier looked around. "Where's the kids?"

"They in the kitchen eating breakfast before the school bus comes to pick them up in an hour. Now what happened? Why are you up so early?"

"I need your advice. I met this kid named Head, who's supposed to know you, a few months back, but I didn't kick it with him. And also Li'l Momma put on blast that I was married. Well, he just called and asked me to breakfast."

Trina remembered Head very well. "Did he tell you I used to fuck with his boss?"

"His boss?"

"Yeah, Nut. You sound surprised. Did he tell you that Nut worked for him?"

"Ma, this isn't about you and Nut. I came down here to ask your advice about me and Head. And, no, he didn't get into who worked for who, because he was too busy flirting with me."

"So what you mean, you came to ask my advice?"

"Should I go?"

"Why the fuck not?"

"I would feel really grimy if anyone saw us together. He wants to meet this morning in East New York. What if Wonderful or Blake see us?"

"What the fuck you got to feel guilty about? After you put up with Jason and his steady stream of bitches? You better tell them to kiss your ass!"

"But you know that it's a double standard. People won't care that Jason was a habitual cheater. They'll forget about him and Monya, and they'll forget that he got shot up in a motel with another mistress. They'll look at me like I'm a slut. Jason hasn't even recuperated, and if they see me out on the prowl, I'll be the slut of Brooklyn."

Trina couldn't believe her ears. "Since when you care about what people think? Or double standards, for that matter? At sixteen you started your own cartel and hugged the block better than most niggas. Now you wanna come in here with fear in your voice over what people say about you? I didn't raise no coward, and you're turning me off right now. I told you back in the day that you're supposed to worry when people *stop* talking about you, because as long as they're yapping their mouths, it means you're doing something right. Fuck those haters. Besides, Wonderful and Blake would never come at you sideways. If they stare you down, then you better stare the fuck back. And if I remember Head correctly, he ain't one to fuck with. If he's feeling you, then he'll hold you down. Look, Jason is the past. He made his bed, so now he has to lie in it."

Cartier had less than twenty minutes to shower and race out the house to drive into East New York to meet with Head. It's amazing what one could do under pressure. She tossed on a pink Juicy Couture sweatsuit that hugged her figure, pulled her hair back into a loose ponytail, and put on a pair of Christian Dior goggle shades to cover any remnants of puffy eyes. She emerged out of her house looking refreshed.

To take the edge off her nerves, she turned on the radio, and Beyoncé's "Single Ladies (Put a Ring on It)" rang through the speakers. Cartier abruptly changed the channel to AM to hear the weather report. She liked Beyoncé as much as the next chick, had even seen her in concert twice, but it was time for her to sit her ass down for a minute. She wondered if Beyoncé would ever get tired of screaming and hopping all around the stage.

As Cartier pulled into the mostly empty parking lot, her heart skipped a few beats. She breathed out, knowing she was surely going to run into someone she knew. With her .25 tucked snugly in her Gucci logo shoulder bag, she held her head high and walked in.

"Cartier, so good to see you," Emanuel the manager greeted her. "I'm so sorry to hear about Jason."

"Thank you, Emanuel. He'll be happy to hear that."

Emanuel had been working there for over a decade, working his way up from bus boy to manager. He adored Jason and his crew because they gave him respect and left great tips to the waiters.

Cartier's eyes scanned the room and landed on Head, tucked away in the far corner, a half-smile on his face. *Damn, this man is sexy*, Cartier thought. He was fine in a manly way. There was a maturity to him that Cartier wasn't used to.

"How's your mother?" Emanuel asked as Cartier lingered.

"Huh? Oh, she's fine."

"Is someone meeting you here this morning?"

"I found who I'm looking for. Thanks, E. I'll tell Jason what you said."

Emanuel's eyes followed Cartier for a moment until he made eye contact with Head. He knew that this wasn't his business and was wise enough to never repeat anything he saw or overheard in the diner.

"I see you got here on time . . . and looking gorgeous I might say."

Cartier blushed. "Why wouldn't I make it on time? I don't live too far from here."

"Because your ass was dead sleep, that's why."

"I was not!"

"Ma, don't ever lie to me. Especially on small things. You lie about small things, then you'll lie about big things, and at the end of the day, you'll never be one to trust. Don't ruin who you are, or what we got by being fake."

"Wait. Slow down. I don't know who you think I am, but you got me fucked up. If I said I wasn't 'sleep, who the fuck are you to tell me differently? And right now you're bugging, talking 'bout what we got. I don't even know you."

"And you won't get to know me." With that, Head stood up, grabbed his *New York Times*, and walked out of the diner, leaving Cartier on the spot.

As Head strolled out of the diner, he knew he had her. If there was one thing he knew was true, it was that once you establish boundaries, you'll always have respect. He told her over the phone that he didn't tolerate lateness, and she showed up on time. Now he had to break her in, train her as one would a dog. He hated to be so harsh, but that was the only way for strong-minded people to learn. He knew from jump that Cartier was a leader with a dominating personality, and that women like her would always bump heads with a man like himself, so to avoid all the future drama, he set them straight from the get-go.

Head felt that Cartier would play the "I-got-a-man-who-spoils-me-I-don't-need-you" role, had he not bounced. Now, she'd be second-guessing all her movements. He would bet his fortune that she'd never had a nigga bounce on her. And although it was a bit dramatic, he knew there were three certain things: death, taxes, and that Cartier would definitely call him.

On the drive back home, Cartier was more than humiliated. She was embarrassed, angry, and felt dumb. She replayed what had happened over and over in her head and still didn't know what hit her. Did she ever think he would play her like that, Cartier Timmons-Payne, the head of The Cartel? Her name was resonating through the streets as well. Who the fuck did this old-school player think he was? This was the second incident she felt she could never live down. The first was Mari pulling a gun on her. Cartier felt like she was slipping. She wasn't thinking on her feet. She should have never run out of the house like she did. He knew she was married, and here she was running out to meet a nigga she'd met once a few months back. How desperate did she look? And who in the world had given him her number?

Cartier didn't want to go right back home because she knew Trina would be all up in her grill. She made a U-turn on Linden Boulevard and drove to the local Pathmark supermarket in downtown Brooklyn just to kill time. From there she cruised back on the block to hang out with Bam and Li'l Momma. Although it was still early, both girls came out, and they headed to Sophie's for a wash and set. Then everyone went their separate ways. Even after hooking up with the girls, Cartier was still breathing fire.

The silence in the luxury vehicle was welcomed as Cartier finally decided to drive home. She wasn't in the mood to listen to lyrics, wanting to get her thoughts together. She had a lot on her plate. As she sat at the red light about to drive through Conduit Boulevard and make her way on to the Belt Parkway, she heard a faint *Pop!*

Then *Pop! Pop! Pop!* Which she ignored, until her back window shattered, scaring the life out of her.

Without even waiting for the light to change, Cartier bolted out in the ongoing traffic. As she raced onto the highway, her head slightly ducked down, she could see what appeared to be a blue Ford Taurus giving chase. But truthfully, right at the moment her hands were trembling. All she wanted to do was get away, and through all the anxiety and angst of the moment, she knew she couldn't lead the perpetrators to where she lived.

With the Taurus still in sight, she began to dip and weave in and out of traffic, headed toward the Southern State Parkway, hoping she'd made the right decision. Within seconds the state trooper was on her ass. Before pulling over on the shoulder, she drove a few more miles to make sure she was no longer being followed, which certainly annoyed the trooper.

Cartier tried to exit the vehicle, but the trooper immediately barked an order for her to stay in her vehicle.

As he approached, clad in his khaki riding pants, holstered gun now drawn, and a look of contempt plastered on his face, Cartier began to tremble. She'd just remembered she was riding dirty. Quickly she opened her purse and slid out her wallet. Showing a sign of respect, she shut down her ignition and held her hands up high and began to cry.

"Officer, I was trying to get your attention!"

"Driving one hundred twenty miles per hour would do exactly that. Step out of the car and put your hands behind your back."

"What? Why?"

"Look, ma'am, step out of the car and put your hands behind your back. You're being arrested for driving eighty miles over the legal speed limit."

"Somebody just tried to kill me and I'm going to jail?"

Finally the angry trooper observed the broken window. "What happened?" The tone in his voice dropped a few octaves.

Cartier needed to lay this on thick. She still had five years on paper, and if she got arrested, they would certainly find her .25, which might be traced back to a murder and attempted murder if the police decided to do a ballistics test.

"I dropped my children off at school and went to run a few errands at the local shopping center. When I came out, I must have interrupted a shootout with some thugs because, before I knew it, I was being shot at." More tears. "I didn't know what to do. When I saw they were still following me, I began speeding, hoping to alert the police and scare them off."

"Exactly where were you?"

"I was just about to get on the Belt Parkway. Oh my God! What if my kids were in the car? They could have been killed."

Cartier looked up and gave the cop full eye contact. Her eyes pleaded for him to believe her partially true story.

"You can put your hands down, ma'am. Sit tight in the car and I'll be back."

The trooper began to walk off but turned back around. Cartier was watching his every move in her side view mirror. Her heart plummeted.

"Are you hurt? Do you need any medical attention?"

"I'm a little shaken up, but no, I'm not shot."

"Did you happen to get the license plate of the vehicle that shot at you?"

"It all happened too fast. There wasn't any way I could get a license plate from my position. I was looking straight ahead, but I can give you an accurate description of the vehicle."

The trooper pulled out his pad. "OK. Could you hand me your license and registration?"

Cartier nodded her head yes and reached for her wallet.

"What type of vehicle was it?"

"A green Nissan Pathfinder. Maybe around a 1992-1998, before they changed the body to resemble the Q-45 truck. Do you know which one I'm talking about?" There wasn't any way Cartier was involving the police in her beef.

For some reason the trooper looked amused. He flashed a smile, softening the hard lines on his mean face.

Cartier sat perched on the shoulder of the Southern State Parkway for another thirty minutes before she was allowed to leave, but not before the trooper casually asked if she would voluntarily submit to popping her trunk, which she was more than happy to do.

Once again she decided to not go home. She needed to get with The Cartel and fill them in on what just gone down and how close she came to getting locked down. First thing on her list was to get rid of her dirty piece. The second thing would be to start burying muthafuckas.

CHAPTER 21

Can I Get a' Encore

The blazing heat outside couldn't compare to how heated Cartier was. After she dropped the car off at the Mercedes dealer to repair the window, she grabbed a loaner car and headed back to Bed-Stuy, where she asked Bam and Li'l Momma to meet her at Janet's house.

Janet welcomed the company. Her weary eyes hadn't been outside her apartment for weeks. She was still grappling over the finality of her daughter's death. She embraced Cartier and led her into the living room, which had seen better days.

"You sounded hype on the phone," Janet said. "Tell me what went down."

"They tryin' to get at me. Muthafuckas just shot out my back window."

"What?" Janet replied, amazed that someone could be so brazen in broad daylight. "Did you get a chance to see who it was?"

"Nah. I only saw the make and model of the car. It was a Ford Taurus with tinted windows."

"Well, you know it was Ryan," Janet deduced. "Even if

he wasn't actually the one bucking shots, he was certainly the one who ordered the hit."

Cartier shook her head as the realization sunk in. All along Jason was supposed to handle Ryan, and now that assignment had shifted to her. She was more than ready to step up to the plate, knowing if she didn't get at Ryan quick, then there would be another funeral for yet another Cartel member.

"I just can't believe that pussy muthafucka is running around ordering hits and murdering people. Ryan was the most bitch nigga anyone could know. Now he's out here like a thoroughbred. He gotta be stopped."

"Y'all fuckin' around," Janet said. "You know the hood says that you don't go to war unless you got your money right. Well, y'all got your money right. Use it to get at that faggot."

"Cartier, as long as Ryan is alive, we're all marked for death. I'm with you on whatever decision you make. A lot is at stake here. Not only did he kill Shanine and Monya, but if he gets at you, then it's only a matter of days before me and Bam are next. He ain't God. He can be stopped too. I can't sit around while this punk decides my date of death," Li'l Momma stated. "Right now, if I'm talking real talk, I'm scared to go home most nights. I'm leery as hell and always looking over my shoulders, waiting for a gun to be tossed in my face."

"I feel you." Cartier took in everyone's worries.

"Put that paper up," Janet said. "Flush him out. Money talks and bullshit walks. Find out where he gets his hair cut, grocery-shops, goes to the gym. Shit, if y'all need me and Trina to beat the block with y'all, you know we're down for whatever. 'Ain't no shook hands in Brookland' has always been our motto. And I'm telling you girls now, I can't go to another funeral. God forbid something happens to any of you girls, I won't be there. I just can't." Janet looked off out the window as her heart broke into a million pieces.

"There won't be any more funerals for The Cartel," Bam finally spoke up. "We're gonna get that bastard. Right, Cartier?"

Cartier nodded her head. "And Marisol, she's gotta get it too."

"Marisol?" Janet wasn't sure where she'd heard the name before. "Is that Ryan's chick?"

"Yeah."

"Oh, well, then I agree, especially after what went down with her sister. Leaving her alive will be a problem."

Cartier was shocked that Janet knew what went down with Jalissa, which meant she knew Cartier was behind what happened to Jason. She'd almost forgotten that Trina and Janet were the best of friends, almost sisters, and didn't keep anything from each other.

"We need to get at Ryan and Marisol together. I got a strong feeling that I can't shake that her need for revenge will be stronger than Ryan's. Sure, Ryan killed our friends, but he had an agenda, and that was to make money. Greed is what will motivate any hustler. Coming at me today was more personal. I don't think I'm high on Ryan's hit list, especially now that Jason is out the way. I'm not saying—and, Bam, please don't chime in—that Ryan isn't a threat and that because we had a fling that he wouldn't dead me. I'm not saying that. I'm saying that there isn't any money involved in murking me. What Ryan did to the Cartel members was business. The attempted hit on me today was personal, and it has Marisol's name written all over it. She's a problem. I know she is. I can feel it in my bones. I saw it in her eyes that she knew I was behind her sister's murder."

"So whatchu saying?" Li'l Momma asked. "That Marisol could have been the one in the Taurus?"

"Maybe, yes. Maybe, no. I'm not sure. But I'm sure that she's the one who will keep the fire lit under our asses. She will stay in Ryan's ear to dead us, just as I stayed in Jason's ear to dead Ryan. We gotta remember that Shanine and Monya were like our sisters. Jalissa *was* her sister."

"Damn, Cartier," Bam began. "You done got us all in some more stupid shit."

Cartier jerked her head back, befuddled. "What are you talking about?" She turned to look at the others. "What is she talking about?"

"She's talking stupid as usual," Li'l Momma exclaimed. "You's one dumb ass, Bam. Now I usually ride with you on certain points, but this isn't Cartier's fault in any way. They chose this beef, and we're gonna finish it. The players are still the same. Ryan's gotta go, and once he is deaded, there would always be the chance that Marisol could be a problem. If not for Jalissa, then she might have come at us for Ryan."

Bam remained silent and the people in the room couldn't read her so they continued with the meeting without her making any further comments.

Janet decided to end the meeting with her parting words of wisdom. "OK, y'all gotta find people, trustworthy people, who work for the telephone company, DMV, collection agencies—anywhere that if you gave them a first and last name you could get an address. Any address that could get you closer to Ryan and Marisol. Once they're gone, the beef will be gone. Y'all won't have to worry about his goons. You know what they say. Hit the biggest nigga in the crew and everyone else will fall. Ryan is that big nigga. Once he falls, his crew will dismantle."

∞

When Cartier finally made it home, she had a nagging feeling to call Head. She told herself that she was only calling to curse him out for playing her. He had called her out of her house then left her looking silly, causing her to almost get killed.

"You owe me an apology!" Her voice was stern yet her heart pumped fearfully. She had no idea how the disrespectful bad boy would react to her ill temper.

"Nah, ma. I see it the other way around."

"How the fuck do I owe you an apology when you walked out on me after I got out of my bed to come and see you?"

"So you were asleep?"

"Huh?" Cartier realized she'd just played herself. Twice.

"Look, shorty, I love the sassy, gangster-bitch thing you got going on. All that bass in your husky voice is sexy as hell. But, as I told you earlier, I don't tolerate a liar. Now you're hitting me on my jack for a reason, as I hit you on yours for a reason. All these antics aren't necessary. Now apologize for lying and we could get up. If not, then peace."

His voice was smooth like butter. He had a swagger that Cartier wanted to get to know better. There was such an excitement building with each second they remained on the phone. Was it because she was still married? The scandalous element to the situation had Cartier wanting more. Briefly she wondered, was this the allure of it all? Cheating? Was this the feeling that Jason couldn't resist?

"OK, I lied," Cartier lowered her voice. "I didn't want you to know that I was asleep. It was stupid, I know, but it wasn't as disrespectful as you walking out on me this morning."

"Disrespect is disrespect. An act you can't measure. And I'm not going to apologize for anything on my end. I'm a man with boundaries. But I forgive you. Now, what's up? You wanna go out tonight? Because I know you didn't really call thinking you were going to get me to say sorry. And before you reply, think about your answer. So tell me, you called because you wanna see me. True?"

Slick mouth, check. Cocky, check. Huge ego, double check. Cartier hesitated briefly. "True."

CHAPTER 22

If This Isn't Love

Cartier came downstairs looking like a movie star, all clad in red—dress, heels, clutch, and lipstick. She felt very trampy, which fit her mood.

"Ma, can you watch the kids for me tonight?"

Trina looked up to see Cartier already dressed, which annoyed her. "Look, Cartier, how do you know I ain't got my own plans?"

"What are you talking about? I'm asking you, not telling you, to watch the kids."

"Don't give me that. You're already dressed and walking out the door. When was you gonna let me know that you were heading out? Just because you put a roof over my head don't mean that I'm your live-in slave. How 'bout all the years I kept a roof over your head?"

"You're my mother. You were supposed to keep a roof over my head! *And* food on the table."

"What's that supposed to mean? Because, if you got a problem with me staying here, I can go back to where I came from. I got my own place, you know. I don't got to be treated like this, all cooped up in here day and night watching all these damn kids, like this is a daycare center. And I'm not getting paid."

"Getting paid? Oh, so now I'm supposed to pay you?"

"Just go, go." Trina swatted Cartier out of her face.

"Anyway, they won't give you a problem. Cee Cee and Jr. will be asleep in a few minutes and should sleep throughout the night."

"Now you know that's a damn lie. Cee Cee wakes up every night hollering for her strawberry milk."

Cartier wondered what was really annoying her mother. "I gave them both a tablespoon of Dimetapp, so as I said, they'll sleep through the night."

Trina exploded. "What did I tell you 'bout drugging those damn kids? Ain't near one of them got a cold. You keep it up, Cartier, and you gonna have two retards on your hands."

"I'll be back before the sun comes up. If you want to go back to Brooklyn tomorrow, feel free. And thanks for asking about how my day went." Cartier stormed out of the house, hoping to leave Trina on a guilt trip.

"Kiss my ass!"

Trina climbed in her bed and lit up a cigarette. "I will go back to Brooklyn and get the hell out of this here prison. Can't have no company," she said to herself. "Always gotta go through all this drama with this ungrateful spoiled brat. Got me living in the middle of a war zone. Shiittt!" Trina rolled her eyes. "I ain't had no dick in months. She must have bumped her fuckin' head, trying to threaten me."

Cartier met Head in Brooklyn and parked her car. From there they drove to Nobu restaurant on Houston Street, where just a few feet from their table sat actress Sandra Bullock. Cartier wasn't a dick-rider, but she was amused to see the actress in person, being somewhat a fan of her work.

As far as the food went, she was disappointed. Years ago, when you couldn't even score a table at the high-priced establishment, the food was scrumptious. Now, her black cod with tempura was too salty, the sake was bitter, and the salad was soggy.

Head wasn't impressed either. "You ready to get out of here?" he asked.

"With pleasure."

Once outside Head clearly didn't want the night to end. Neither did Cartier.

"So are you ready to head home, or can you hang out a little more?"

"I can hang." She hoped he couldn't read her eagerness.

"That's a good look. So where are we heading? Do you want to go and grab a drink somewhere?"

"I definitely need a strong drink after my day."

Head kept his Cayenne parked in the garage on Houston because he no longer felt like driving, so the pair caught a taxi to the W Hotel on Union Square. The hotel's restaurant lounge area was packed, even though it was almost midnight. New York was certainly the city that never sleeps.

"I hear they make an amazing Bellini, you know, a chick drink."

Pangs of jealousy shot through Cartier's veins. How many women had he brought there to sip on Bellini? Instead of saying something and sounding immature, she remained silent.

Once seated at the bar, Cartier ordered the usual, "Apple martini."

Three drinks later, Head revisited Cartier's earlier remark. "You said you had a bad day. I'm not going to presume that it had anything to do with me, but if it did, then I hope I'm making up for it."

Cartier tilted her head to the side and shrugged her shoulders, trying to shake off the day's events. "Well, it did start off bad because of you. I felt really disrespected, but I got over that quickly. Today almost ended with me in a pine box."

"Come again?"

"Yeah, shit got ugly out there for me today. I was on my way home, and someone just started bucking shots at me."

"You sure it was meant for you?"

"I'm one hundred."

"So you got a beef?"

"Something like that." Cartier tried to downplay the situation.

"Well, what about your husband?"

"What about your girl?"

It was now Head's turn to tilt his head to one side. He had no idea where the conversation was going. He wanted to know if the beef was her husband's beef, or at least, would he handle it. There wasn't any way he could sit back and let his wife, or even his girl, handle any beef.

"What's that about?"

"You tell me," Cartier replied.

Head got the hint. "You wanna take this upstairs?"

"Maybe . . ." Cartier paused for effect. She couldn't believe she was being so forward. Although she had been drinking, she was far from drunk, so there wouldn't be any blaming it on the alcohol. "What about your girl?"

Head chuckled. "Shorty, you don't got shit to worry about. Old girl and I are done. There won't be any encores."

"That's what they all say."

"I'm sure the average nigga does say fairytale shit like that, but I'm a real dude. If I say something, then you can always take it at face value. My girl left me when I was locked down. She didn't even stay around long enough to be there for my sentencing. She thought a nigga was finished. She knew I was facing more lives than a cat, so she walked. I knew she wasn't shit when we hooked up. She was my man Nut's girl, and when he got murked, she slid on over my way."

"Damn! That's fucked up."

"No doubt. On both our parts. I was just as grimy as her. I was a little young nigga and thought she represented something because she was fucking around with the head nigga in charge. I don't really blame her for her actions, though. She was a street chick who was only exposed to that fast life, fast money, fast niggas. It comes with the territory."

"Did Trina know her? It seems like this Nut got around."

"I don't know, maybe. But Trina and Nut was more like a fling. And any young nigga getting paper is gonna get around, ma."

"So you don't care that she didn't do your bid with you?"

"Nope."

"You must still love her then."

"As I said, I understand her actions. I got love for her, but I would never love her again. We're done. I'm not a man who makes the same mistake twice."

Cartier assumed that, in his roundabout way, he was saying he was a free agent. She wanted to be the right chick to pull him off the market.

While Head got the room, Cartier ordered one last drink for the road only. She needed something stronger than the apple martini. Quickly, she gulped down the double shot of Hennessy. All at once she was shy, horny, adventurous, and also ready to put her marriage behind her, which meant erasing Jason's as the last dick she'd fucked.

They'd only been in the room for a few minutes before Cartier's head began to spin.

Head noticed immediately as she wobbled, trying to take off her stilettos. "Are you all right?"

"I'm fine. Just got a little lightheaded, that's all."

"Come here." Head motioned for her to have a seat on the side of the plush mattress. "Let me help you with these."

After Cartier took a seat, Head bent down on his knees and gently removed her shoes. "You have pretty feet." He admired her small foot as it sat daintily in his large hands. When he looked up, he saw Cartier's dilated eyes. "Are you sure you're OK?"

"I told you I'm fine," she whispered, and then began a chest-rattling cough.

"You don't look fine. You need to lie down. You've definitely had too much to drink."

Suddenly, Cartier had the urge to throw up. As Head got up to call room service for bottled water and milk to help coat her stomach, she ran past him and just barely made it to the toilet and regurgitated.

Head was right on her heels as she kneeled over the toilet to throw up virtually everything she'd eaten all day. As her stomach muscles churned and contracted, and her insides seared her throat, Cartier thought she was going to die from the pain.

As she sat crouched over the toilet, helpless, looking a hot mess, Head rubbed her back soothingly.

Cartier held her head over the toilet for almost an hour, with spurts of vomit every ten to twenty minutes. She knew she should have never mixed her drinks, but she was slightly nervous about screwing Head, not to mention he was somewhat intimidating.

Finally, when she tried to stand up, her knees wobbled and then buckled. Head caught her and picked her up and took her straight to the bed. He laid her down and tossed the down comforter on top of her.

He stood there for a moment staring at the sickly woman, not knowing exactly what he could do to help her feel better. When room service came with the water and milk, he sent them back to bring her some soup. He knew she needed something in her stomach because she'd surely emptied it with all that vomiting.

He put his hand over her forehead. "You're burning up."

Head went in the bathroom and got a cool cloth to wipe her forehead, only to return to a sleeping beauty. Next, he began undressing her, and as he slid off the red silk dress, the gun fitted snugly to her thigh took him by surprise. The sexy temptress with the toned body, baby-soft skin, and sassy attitude was packing a piece. Clad in only her lace bra and panties, this girl kept Head's dick brick-hard.

He removed her gun and covered her back up. "Cartier, wake up, ma."

Cartier struggled to open her eyes. Her vision was blurry, and her head was pounding. She knew where she was and who she was with, but all she wanted to do was close her eyes in hopes that the pain would go away. She hadn't been that fucked up in years. Not since she was a teenager trying to be grown. She knew she'd definitely played herself.

"Drink this. It'll make you feel better." Head placed the cup of milk in her hands, and she took a sip. "No, you gotta drink it all."

Cartier wanted to smack the cup out of his hand because she was in so much pain. Instead she exhaled and forced herself to drink the room-temperature milk. He followed by feeding her a bowl of soup.

Once she was done, Cartier was allowed to finally go to sleep. Head nestled up behind her, his massive hand resting on her flat stomach.

Cartier awoke to the television on in the room, but she didn't see Head. Draped only in her bra and panties, she wondered if they'd fucked and he bounced. She reached down and felt her vagina, which seemed fine, untouched. She wanted to call for him, but her throat was still on fire.

She peeked over at the clock, which said nine thirty. Cartier knew Trina was going to lose her mind and curse her out the moment she walked through the door. Briefly she toyed with the idea of calling her mother to let her know she'd be home soon but quickly decided against it. Why get cursed out twice? She'll just swallow her medicine when she got home.

Shortly thereafter, Head came back into the room with breakfast. Cartier's heart was flying around in her chest. She was relieved that he was still around.

He walked in the room, bringing the aroma of sweet maple syrup and coffee with him. "How are you feeling?"

"Much better." Cartier lied unconvincingly.

"You don't look OK." Head checked her forehead for a fever. When his hands slid down to her neck, she was soaked in sweat. "Stay here, I'm going to run you a bath."

As the water was running, he pulled open the drapes in the hotel room to let the sunshine in. He then handed her a breakfast of pancakes, scrambled eggs, and toast. "Here, eat this first and then you can bathe. Make sure you drink all of that milk I got for you, and take those Advils. It should help you to get your strength back."

After Cartier ate most of her breakfast and took the Advils, she honestly felt better. Her head fog lifted, and she wanted to resume where they'd left off last night.

Head, still treating her like a patient, walked her into the bathroom and sat down on the toilet stall. "Come here."

Cartier walked in between his legs. When he reached up and began to take off her panties, she took one step back. "What are you doing?"

"I'm getting ready to bathe you. You're all sweaty, and this should make you feel a little better. And don't go getting all shy on me. You're practically naked anyway, standing here with those little teeny-weeny see-through panties on."

Cartier burst out into laughter. "Shouldn't we be leaving soon? Isn't checkout at noon?"

"Re-lax, ma. I paid for another night. I didn't know if you'd be well enough to make it home, and I didn't want to drag my lady out of here half-dead."

"Is that the only reason you paid for another night?"

"I thought it was, but it seems you got a better reason for us to stay another night."

Gently, Head reached up and slid off Cartier's bra down her shoulders, and it fell to the floor. She was now standing in front of Head completely naked, and she didn't even flinch. As Head's strong, masculine hands brushed up against her skin, Cartier watched as he studied her perky breasts, his eyes lingering on her cropped pussy hair, and finally her perfect French-pedicured feet.

Head put both hands on her hips and guided her inside the Jacuzzi-shaped tub. "How's the water? Is it too hot?" he asked.

"No, it's perfect," Cartier's voice was barely a whisper as her pussy throbbed excitedly.

Head grabbed the washcloth and soap and began at her feet. He lathered the rag and began to wash between her toes in slow, strong strokes. Then he moved from her calves to her upper thigh, kneading his fingers in small circular movements, which almost caused Cartier to have an orgasm. The foreplay was that intense.

When his shirt got wet from bath water, he stood up and pulled his white T-shirt over his head. His broad shoulders, firm pecs, and ripe nipples complemented his small waist and flat stomach.

"Stand up," he said to Cartier, and then he kneeled down.

Hesitantly she rose to her feet and stood, her pussy in Head's face. Tenderly, he separated her legs and took the washcloth and began cleansing her inner thighs in circular motions, slowly inching toward her cave.

Head, an experienced lover, took the tip of the rag and parted Cartier's lips, and applied pressure, and as his fingers brushed her clitoris in a steady, firm motion, she gripped his shoulders tight, trying to stop herself from quivering.

Head's eyes met hers, and he held her stare for a long moment before a sly grin spread across his face. "That feel good?"

Cartier could only nod her head. When she peeked down at his jeans, she could see a slight bulge.

Head wanted to caress and make love to Cartier's whole body and mind. He moved up to her arms, fingers, and the nape of her neck, before making his way to her breasts. As soon as the intensity was overbearing, he would pull back momentarily, teasing her. Head released the water from the tub and turned on the shower, allowing the water to drench the suds from Cartier's body.

As she stood there, water cascading down her body, Head began pulling off his jeans, boxers, and then socks and stood before her completely naked. It was then Cartier noticed that he had a heavy penis that hung between bow legs. She moved over to make room for him in the shower.

Neither one of them said a word as he reached for the shampoo and began lathering her scalp. His strong fingers stroked her scalp as if he was making love to her.

At first, Cartier didn't want to get her hair wet. But that was a fleeting thought as he tilted her head back and allowed the water to cascade down on her hair. She closed her eyes, Head's hands supporting the back of her neck.

Head pulled her head up, surprising her when he leaned in and kissed her lips softly. Cartier eyes popped open.

And then he kissed her again, this time more aggressively, her enthusiastic lips welcoming him. Cartier's tongue snaked inside his mouth, and they both began to grope one another passionately.

"We shouldn't be doing this," Cartier breathed.

"Yes, we should . . ."

"But you won't respect me." Suddenly Cartier began to worry.

"You don't have to earn my respect, ma. I'll give it to you. But remember it's on you to lose it."

Cartier nodded her acknowledgment and all apprehensions were washed away.

Both soaked and slippery, Head carried her to the bed and gently laid her down.

Finally he spoke as he climbed on top of her. "I've been wanting to make love to you from the first moment I saw you."

"You've been on my mind too." She reached up for him.

They started off slowly with long, deep kisses as he dug his hands in her damp hair. Head sucked and licked her nipples until they looked like two copper nickels.

Cartier moaned as his strong hands groped her body. As he began to nibble passionately on her neck, she squealed with delight.

After putting on a condom, Head pressed his dick against the opening of her pussy and applied a controlled pressure. As Cartier's vagina resisted, he pushed harder, until the tip burst through. He teased her for a minute, just rocking his tip in and out. As her pussy walls opened wider, he sank deeper inside her juicy cave, his strong pelvis rocking back and forth, keeping a steady rhythm.

As he gently made love to her, the moment felt surreal. Was she really in a hotel room having an affair, getting slayed lovely by a perfect stranger?

As the moment intensified, she wrapped her legs around Head's waist, and they both gripped each other tightly.

"I'm getting ready to cum," he murmured. "Ahhhhh, I'm cumming."

"Me too," she crooned.

As Head came, he whispered in her ear, "You got a nigga whipped."

Cartier felt euphoric. "That was so good."

Head chuckled, "I know a few positions…"

CHAPTER 23

Doing It and Doing It Well

One day later, Head and Cartier were still held up in the hotel, cell phones off, tuning out the world. Cartier knew it was reckless and irresponsible, but she couldn't see past her selfish needs to care about others, and for the moment, that included her kids. She knew they were in good hands with her mother. She just needed this escape from all the drama and a broken marriage.

For hours Cartier droned on and on about her worries—marriage, kids, Trina, Monya, Shanine, their beef, and her current circumstance.

"So who's the kid y'all got beef with?"

"His name is Ryan."

"Ryan? From where?"

"He's from Harlem. You heard of him?"

Head seemed to hesitate. "Nah, not at all."

"Well, what's messed up is that he and I used to kick it back in the day, and I thought he was cool with all The Cartel members. I know that's why they had their guard down, on the strength of my relationship with him, and look how that turned out."

Head gave Cartier a long, sensual kiss. "You're putting too much blame on your shoulders. Spread some of that guilt around. Shanine and Monya made their own choices, and so did Ryan."

"What are we doing? I'm risking everything, and I don't know if, when you walk out of that door, I'll see you again. Is this just a sex thing?"

"Well, ask me then."

"Will I? Am I going to see you again?"

"As long as you need me, I'm here for you. From the first moment I saw you, I wanted you. Something pulled me to you, and that doesn't happen often."

"Speaking of our first meeting, how did you get my number when I didn't give it to you?"

"I have my resources." Head smiled cockily.

"So you're not going to tell me?"

Head shook his head no, torturing the curious Cartier but also leaving her intrigued.

"But why me?"

"Why not you? Please don't let me find out you're insecure, because I'm telling you now, you don't have a reason to be."

"Nah, it's not that. But you know it's hard for me to put my feelings into another man. I did that with my husband, and he slept with my best friend. I want to know that if I give you my heart, you won't break it. That I can always be myself and not have to put on."

"That's what I wanted from you from jump. Remember you wanted to start off lying about whether or not you were 'sleep. Ma, that's petty. I always want you to be yourself and keep it one hundred."

"So you'd be able to accept me and all my baggage? My two kids and crazy mother, the whole nine?"

"Cartier, listen. There aren't too many dudes out here like me. I play by all the rules. Under the tutelage of Nut, I learned a lot. Unfortunately, I didn't fully comprehend what he was trying to drill into my thick skull until it was almost too late. I was lucky. I got another shot. My man didn't get the same chance I got. He had a good girl who went down for the count. She's doing life now in a fed pen because she didn't give him up. That shit broke his heart, but he moved on and hooked up with Tawana. I want a girl who would do a bid for me, but I also want to be the man who would never allow my girl to do a bid for me. What Jason got you in, this beef with this Ryan kid, ain't how I would have handled things. I would have tucked you and my family safely away and not let you out until Ryan and everyone he loved was dead."

"He was trying his hardest to get at—"

"That's bullshit, baby girl. It doesn't take a year to dead anyone. Not even the President of the United States. You told me he said make sure you go out each day with your pistol. If you were mines, I wouldn't ever want you to touch that steel. You're a lady."

"But I was handling mines way before I hooked up with him. He didn't create a gangster chick; he married one."

"Well, I'ma marry a lady. And although I love your

gangster, after a while it wears thin and that ride or die pledge was only for the moment, not a lifetime. I'm looking for somebody to wife who isn't all consumed about being seen in the streets with the biggest nigga on the block."

Cartier pouted. Was he saying that she wasn't good enough for him to marry?

"Good luck on finding your trampy lady to marry."

"Why she gotta be a tramp? Just because she gave me her goodies on the first night certainly doesn't make her a tramp."

"Ohh." Cartier's smile stretched a mile. "You mean me?"

"I should hope so."

"But you don't even know me. And I'm married."

"Divorce dude. He's lame anyway."

Cartier leaned over and gave him a soft kiss. "And what about Tawana?"

Head returned the kiss and began massaging her lower back. "I would have never approached you if there was still a her and me. That part of my life is over. I'm hoping to start a new chapter with you."

Head raised his hands and began to gently pinch Cartier's nipples. She was naked, except for her Omega watch. And he was lying on his back, naked as well, on top of the comforter.

"Your skin is so soft." He removed his hands, propped behind his head, a large grin spreading across his face. "Hey, wifey," he said.

"Hi, daddy," she purred and rubbed up against him.

Slowly she slid down and began kissing from the base of his ankle, his calves, behind his knees, and once she reached his pelvis, his dick was standing at attention. Cartier smiled, opened her mouth, and engulfed his large black penis.

Cartier knew Head had that good dick. The type of penis that got you wet by just looking at it. He didn't even have to touch her, and she was oozing with excitement. No wonder he didn't have to convince her to lay up with him. After making love to Jason's average-sized penis, Cartier felt like she'd been eating tofu for years, and now she was chowing down on steak.

She played around with the tip, nibbling at first. Then she began to deep-throat his massive penis. Her mouth went up and down, her saliva leaving traces that she'd been there.

Head began to rock his pelvis out of sheer pleasure and dug his hands into Cartier's layered hairstyle.

In between licks, she said, "It feel good, daddy?"

"Damn, baby! You fuck me so good."

"You like this?" She jerked his dick with her hands, sucking the tip.

"Ohhhh, yes-s-s!"

Cartier continued to give Head a blowjob, occasionally peeking up at him to see the look of pleasure plastered on his face.

"I'm about to cum," he moaned. "I'm about to cum."

Head exploded inside her mouth, and as the hot juices entered her throat, she swallowed every bit of it until he was done. She felt so freaky and hot, she was beyond cooling down.

Immediately, Head flipped her over, spread her legs wide, and began to taste her pussy juices. He sucked on her clit until he heard her moan in pleasure. Then he began to gently nibble and bite down on her clitoris, while his two fingers explored her vagina.

Cartier began to grind her hips in slow motion, getting lost in the moment. When it started getting really good to her, she took his head and smashed his face in her pussy and grinded harder.

"Your pussy tastes sweeter than candy."

"Eat it all up, daddy."

"No doubt."

Soon after, Head wrapped up his penis, mounted Cartier and eased into her slippery pussy and began to hit her G-spot with precision. Cartier's French manicure dug into his muscular back as they came together. Intertwined between Cartier's toned legs, the newly bonded drifted off into a peaceful sleep.

CHAPTER 24

Soap Opera Drama

Trina hated to be interrupted when she was watching her soap operas. It was her only time of the day to relax before the kids came home from school. Aimlessly, she answered the phone but didn't say a word. She was too busy hanging on to Erica Kane's every word.

"Hello?" the male caller said.

"Yeah."

"Trina?"

"Yeah, who's this?" Trina asked. Only, she truly didn't care.

"Where's your daughter?" the now familiar voice demanded.

"Jason?"

"Yo, tell Cartier I'm getting out of here soon and I want my Benz, and y'all better get the fuck outta my house. And tell her grimy ass—"

"You know I'm not going to pass no message like that!"

"I want y'all outta my house, yo! Now, I'm asking nicely. A nigga ain't fucked up no more."

"Jason, I think the person you need to be talking to

is—Hello? Hello?"

The phone went dead.

Trina jumped up and ran to the front parlor and peered out the window. Was Jason out the hospital? Was he going to kick in the door, blazing?

After going through the house and checking all doors and windows, she was startled when she heard keys jangling. She was too far from her room to get the gun she kept underneath her mattress, so she ran to the kitchen and grabbed a butcher's knife. With the knife held high, Trina hid near the butler's pantry until she heard the faint clicking of heels. She exhaled and placed the knife back down.

"Cartier, come in here, now!"

"What's up?" Cartier didn't pick up the panic or urgency in her mother's voice, but when they were eye to eye, she knew something was terribly wrong.

"Jason just called here beefing. He said he's getting out the hospital and he wants us out of here and that he also wants his ride."

"Fuck that nigga. I don't give a fuck what he wants! His cripple ass got a lot of nerve, barking orders. He should know by now, fear don't pump through these veins."

"I know I ain't raise no punk, but we're both playing with fire. Jason don't sound in his right mind. And you're forgetting one thing."

"What's that?"

"He knows where we live."

"Ma, we changed all the locks."

"And? What does that mean? All he gotta do is lay low outside and fill you with just as many holes as you filled him with."

"He ain't gonna do shit."

Cartier was full of bravado. She and Head were going strong, and he'd promised that he wasn't going to let anything happen to her.

"Now tell me again, what did he say?"

"Cartier, come sit down." Trina pulled out the kitchen chair. "I've always supported the decisions that you've made, even if they were emotional or foolish decisions. I think you need to stop taking everyone for granted."

Cartier plopped down in the seat. "How am I taking people for granted?"

"I told you that you need to finish what you started. I'm too old to be wondering each night I lay my head down to sleep if I'm going to wake up in the morning. And I'm too old to be worrying about whether or not when I open the door to let my kids or grandkids out for school, if they're going to get hit with a barrage of bullets meant for either you or me."

"Ain't nothing gonna—"

"Shut up!" Trina yelled, quieting Cartier instantly. "And listen to what I have to say. Now you've made a mess, and you need to fix it. You made the decision to try and kill Jason, and you fucked up. My advice was to drain the nigga and run his pockets, but you chose a different route. I'm telling you, you gotta dead Jason, and do it fast. He's a loose end, Cartier, and I can't have our lives in his hands while he decides whether or not he's going to seek revenge. And what about Ryan? And now this new Marisol chick? You getting sloppy. I can feel that something is going to happen."

Cartier still resented what Jason had done to her, but she honestly couldn't imagine having the hate, courage, and gumption to pull the trigger on him once again. In fact, she was emphatic that she couldn't do it a second time, unless she was backed into a corner. Right now she was on a different mission. Falling for Head had taken her focus off of Jason. Head was slowly repairing her broken heart. If Jason was ready to call it a truce, for the sake of the kids, then so was she.

"I think you're blowing this way out of proportion. First, I'm not getting sloppy. I'm still being alert, riding with my pistol, and also circling the block before I walk through here. And with the state of the art surveillance system, we're as protected as we could be in here. The only place I'm vulnerable is on the streets, and with Head holding me down, not too many muthafuckas are going to try me."

"So you got him open?"

"For sure."

"Does he know about the beef with Ryan?"

"Yeah, we kicked it about that."

"And what did he say? That he's going to hold you down?"

"Nah, he said more than that. He said that he's going to inherit my beef."

"And what about Jason?"

"He said he's going to handle all my beefs."

"And are you sure he's to be trusted?"

Cartier nodded her head. "Yeah, I trust him. Why? Because if he was planted by Ryan, we would already be dead. Having said that, I'm still alert and keeping one eye open. After what Jason did to me, I don't think I will ever fully trust anyone but you. But I can't go around always leery either. That's no way to live."

"Well, that makes me feel a little better, but you still got to close up all these loose ends. Go and see Jason and see what's really good. If he's all talk and no action, then Head might be able to give him a pass. If he still got larceny in his heart, then lullaby his ass."

Cartier did as she was told and hopped back in the Benz to go and see Jason. She truly hoped he was ready to throw in the towel. When she walked into the rehabilitation center, she was startled by his appearance. Although it was clear that he'd lost weight from before he got shot, he no longer looked emaciated. He'd definitely gotten his weight back up. The metal wire and cast were removed, and he now had full use of his hands, evident from the fun he was having with a video game on an X-box.

When he noticed Cartier standing there, all the excitement from winning in the game drained from his face. "What the fuck you doing here?"

"You tell me."

Jason stared Cartier from head to toe with contempt and then tossed his control to the floor. "You don't gotta run up here now. I told Trina that I want y'all out of my house."

"And go where?"

"You can go to hell, for all I care. Oh, my bad, that's where you thought *I* was going, right? Isn't that what you said? Fuck that bitch in hell? Like it's some resort or something." Jason grimaced. "Like muthafuckas wanna be in hell fucking bitches."

Cartier laughed. "So you're really saying you want to kick your kids out of the house?"

"Cartier, you're not really getting it. I don't give a fuck about you. You're dead to me. Fucking dead. Do you hear me, bitch?"

Cartier was really trying to contain her anger, but the *bitch* word struck a chord. "Look, I'm here to drop off your car, but you can forget about me and the kids getting out of our house. This is what happens when you cheat on your wife—you lose the house and custody of your kids."

"Ain't this a bitch!" Jason snorted in disgust. "You coming in here like you're an angel, when I hear you got a nigga up under your hood."

"Excuse me?"

"Tell that nigga when I get outta here, I'ma see him too."

"Oh, now you adding more people to your hit list?" Cartier laughed, though somewhat surprised Jason knew about her and Head.

Jason's eyes hooded over in anger, and he bit the inside of his lip, a habit he'd had for years. He half-hoped that she would deny the affair, as he would have done, or at least look like she was sorry.

But the woman who stood before him looked like she didn't have a care in the world, was bursting with happiness. That was something he couldn't accept. He'd spent four months in a rehabilitation center being stuck with needles and swallowing meds while she was out on the streets getting her freak on. Jason couldn't understand why he felt more contempt for Cartier and her new man than anger for her filling him with bullets. Every time his mind wandered to the things Head could be doing to his wife, an inexplicable madness would come over him.

"Keep thinking you got the upper hand. You waltzing in here like you a rock star, when you look like you got a disease you can't get rid of. You don't look as cute as you think you look. I heard that nigga dick you swallowing got the monster!"

Jason's jealousy didn't sway Cartier. She knew he was grasping at straws. "Now you know how it feels to be on the receiving end. And each time Head pushes his large dick into me, ironically I thank you 'cause, had you not fucked up, I would have never got to experience a real man."

"A real man, huh?" Jason's laugh was coarse and filled with anguish. "I had more pussy than—"

"Oh, grow up!" Cartier scolded. "No one cares. . ."

"I should have never looked for qualities in you that I knew never existed. I mean, you fucked my baby momma. What kind of shit was you on?"

"And she was also better in bed than you. So thank

you for that one as well."

Jason couldn't believe his ears. He was sure his last remark would have caused her to grimace but she kept going hard.

"You comin' in here talkin' tough 'cause a nigga ain't one hundred yet."

"No one's going on that sympathy tour with you. You're pathetic."

"Pathetic?" Jason snorted. "Ma, please believe me when I tell you that you have less than a week to relocate. I won't give you the same warning twice."

"Jay, if you were going to do something to me, there wouldn't be any warnings. You move in silence, remember?"

That Cartier had pulled Jason's punk card infuriated him beyond control. In one swift movement, he'd leapt from the bed and wrapped his hands firmly around her neck and began to squeeze with such force and intensity, his weak arm began to throb, but he didn't care. He didn't need a gun to kill Cartier. Her arrogance had provoked him beyond his wildest imagination. He wanted to squeeze until her eyes popped out of her head. Then he wanted to stomp her guts out and make her feel the pain he was feeling.

Cartier's knees felt like marshmallows, and she went limp in Jason's hands. Desperately she tried to scratch and pull at his face, but she was losing oxygen rapidly. Just before she blacked out, she felt Jason release her, and she collapsed on the cold tiles. Cartier sucked in as much air as she could.

Briefly she thought about lifting up her skirt and pulling out her new .25 and finishing what she started, but she just couldn't. Instead, she tossed him the keys to his car. "We'll be gone before you get out of here!"

"You're saying that like you're doing me a favor. Getting out of my house is only part of it. You better leave town, because this beef ain't over until I say it's over!"

"I came here thinking that maybe we could squash this beef for the sake of our kids, but I see you wanna play rough. You can't see past your own selfish vendetta. You and I can deal with each other when you come out. If that means exchanging bullets until the best shot wins, then so be it, but, in the meantime, I still need to get at Ryan and Marisol."

Jason had literally forgotten about the Ryan situation after Cartier had ambushed him in the motel. He still couldn't understand why she just wouldn't let it go. Shanine and Monya were dead and buried, and the last thing on his mind was going after Ryan. Head was now at the top of his list.

"I'ma tell you something I should have told you a long time ago. I don't give a fuck about no Ryan. He was never a priority for me."

The revelation stunned Cartier. Once again, just when she thought she knew Jason, he'd say or do something that made her question how she could have fallen in love with such a selfish man. It was always about his needs and his needs only.

"Again, what about your kids? Are they a priority?"

"Stop bringing up my kids, because you know what they mean to me."

"Do they mean more to you than your mistress? Huh? Because if that's true, then I need an address on Marisol. And each second you think about whether or not to give it to me, your kids are in danger."

"What are you talking about? Stop talking in riddles. I'm sick of this soap opera drama."

Cartier was seething. Slowly she stood to her feet to face Jason, the negative energy percolating around the room.

"The other day I was chased down the parkway with our kids in the car. They shot the car—"

"What? What the fuck you say?"

"That's right. They shot your car up in broad daylight with the kids in the back seat," she lied. "We all could have been killed, and you're saying Ryan was never a priority to you? Had you concentrated on taking him out, instead of fucking Jalissa, you wouldn't have two traumatized kids at home."

Jason went berserk, screaming and throwing wild punches in the air.

Cartier watched the process with trepidation. She'd never seen him so angry. He was foaming at the mouth. But she welcomed his anger. She needed him to want to kill Ryan with as much urgency as she had. Between her, The Cartel, Head, and now Jason gunning for Ryan and Marisol, she felt secure that she wouldn't have to continually look over her shoulders.

"Meet me at your mom's house tomorrow around six. And bring The Cartel. I'll make some calls and bring in Wonderful and Blake. We're gonna flush them out. And get the fuck out of that house today. Not because of me. I don't know what they know. You said some Hispanics ran up in the crib once. I dunno; Jalissa could have been setting me up all along."

Cartier didn't have any intention of getting out of her five-bedroom mansion. Ever. Especially since there weren't any Hispanic burglars. She wanted to make Jason feel guilty about the Jalissa situation. Up until that moment, he hadn't shown any remorse. Instead of hitting him with a barrage of insults, she remained silent and let her glare do all the talking.

Cartier left the hospital with mixed feelings about whether or not to trust Jason. She decided that even if he hated her and loved Jalissa, under no circumstances would he want anything to happen to his kids. So until Ryan and Marisol were dead, she was sure he would now make them a priority. She wasn't stupid enough to trust him with her life, but the life of their kids was a whole different ballgame.

And if Jason even looked like his trigger finger was itching in the wrong direction, she was prepared to finish what she'd started.

CHAPTER 25

Justify My Thug

The two men met in a secluded area at an exclusive golf course in Mahwah, New Jersey. Head's caddy drove him to the ninth hole, where his guest was patiently awaiting his arrival. Clad in white-and-blue golf shoes, Izod pullover, and khaki shorts, Head smiled graciously as he extended his hand for a shake.

"It's been a while, man."

"True indeed." Head pulled out a Cuban cigar and lit it. He wasn't one who smoked daily; only when he felt a need to relax and enjoy life. "I should get at you for not coming to see me as soon as I got out."

"Shit was thick out here. I was trying to get up with you, but you know . . ."

Head looked at him sideways. "You lucky I don't pump three in you right now for not holding me down while I was locked up."

"What?" His guest's eyes popped open in surprise. "I hit you off each month with that paper."

Head shook his head in acknowledgment. "That's not what I needed. I had my own money. I needed my family there for me. You know when Nut got murdered you became like a nephew to me, and I vowed to always look out for you. I had to hear about your come-up from muthafuckas who didn't even know you."

"I feel you, man, but it's not like I keep a nine-to-five. A nigga dirty, and I didn't want to be running to no fed joint."

Head looked deeply into his eyes and saw his sincerity. "So, yo, what are we going to do about this problem?"

Ryan shook his head rapidly. "You know Marisol wants Cartier dead. She thinks that she murked Jalissa."

"She did."

"That's what I thought. Until she's gone, Marisol won't let me rest. All day and all night she keeps hounding me."

"And Cartier wants you dead. Not only does she want revenge for her clique, but now she feels her life is in jeopardy."

"Yo, I didn't have anything to do with what happened to shorty the other day. That was all Marisol. And, truth be told, she's going sick because she missed."

Head exhaled and blew a cloud of smoke in the air. The sweet-tasting cigar had quenched his craving. "So, you gotta keep Marisol in check, and I'll handle Cartier."

"What about Jason?"

"Fuck that nigga!" Head spat. "He lightweight. I'm about to get at him any day if he don't keep his distance."

"Nah, let me handle duke. Been waiting to get at him for a minute now, but ever since Cartier tried to flat-line him, I can't find him."

"That's what I'm here for. He's over at Rosa Parks Rehabilitation Center up in the Bronx."

"That nigga that close?"

"Hell yeah." Head tossed the hundred-dollar cigar after only a few tokes. He then put on his fitted leather gloves and pulled out a number five golf club.

"Ryan, don't take our relationship for granted. Once you put Jason to rest, you and Marisol gotta bounce outta state."

"No doubt."

"Where are you going to take her?"

"Florida. I bought a phat-ass crib down there. Plush enough for her to forget about her sister."

"Yo, how did you feel about Jalissa fucking Jason right under your nose? That nigga could have slumped you."

Ryan pounded his fist into his palm. "I think about that shit every day. I was so mad when I found out, I went upside Marisol's head. She swears she didn't know about it, but that's too hard to believe."

"Of course, she knew. Broads tell each other when they're going to the bathroom."

There was a pregnant pause as the two men thought briefly about their ladies.

"So you really feeling Cartier, huh?"

Head smiled. "That's my heart."

"Yeah, she's cool, but you know I like them Puerto Rican mommies." Ryan downplayed his relationship with Cartier, careful not to say an ill word.

"You like anything with a big ass. Who you foolin'?"

Ryan laughed. "Yeah, that too."

"So when's your departure date?"

"We're jetting in two days. I told Marisol that Cartier would be taken care of tonight."

Head took a healthy swing and hit the ball, which flew very close to the tenth hole. "You know after today we'll never kick it again."

Ryan lowered his head as nostalgic memories came gushing back. He knew that as long as they both chose the woman they loved, they'd have to keep their relationship a secret. If Marisol knew that Ryan's "uncle" was fucking with Cartier, that Ryan wasn't going to kill him because Cartier was off limits, she'd flip. And if Cartier knew Ryan was like a "nephew" to Head, and that he was untouchable, even after he'd killed Shanine and Monya, she'd lose it as well. There would never be any peace. When Head had called and told him—not asked him—to relocate, Ryan knew he only had one choice.

That night Head came to get Cartier at her home to take her to dinner. He said he'd found out a few things, and that they'd kick it in person, not on the phone. When he pulled up on a Ducati motorcycle, the whole neighborhood could hear his engine roaring down the block.

Cartier had no idea he was riding a bike and flung her front door open in complete and utter surprise. Head parked his bike and seemed to pose on it for a few seconds, so Cartier could get the full effect. The black bike with green and yellow trim was beautiful.

"What are you doing?" Cartier asked as she walked toward him.

"I'm here to get my girl and take her out on the town."

"On that?"

"Scared?"

Cartier grinned. "Never."

"Good. Now show me in, so I can see your moms." Head walked through the door.

Cartier watched his eyes scan his surroundings. He didn't say anything, but she knew he was impressed. Her home would impress almost anyone.

Trina heard his voice and came waltzing out of her room in full diva regalia. You would have thought she was going to a nightclub. When Cartier had left this morning, Trina's naturally brown hair, mixed with a few grays, were peeking out, leaving only a few inches of her dyed blonde hair on the tips. Now, her blonde color was fresh, clothes dipped, and her enthusiasm unmatched.

"How in the hell have you been?" she squealed, opening her arms for a full embrace.

Head gave Trina a big bear hug and swung her around. He stood back and examined her. "You still looking good."

Trina blushed. "Come in, come in. Have a seat, and tell me what's been going on since the last time I saw you."

"Ma, we don't have time for all of that."

"What are you talking about?"

"We're going out to dinner."

"I know, Cartier, damn. You can't spare five minutes?"

"You're asking him to recap the past twenty years, so no, I don't have five minutes."

Head could feel some drama coming on. "Don't worry about it, Trina. When we get back, I'll kick it with you."

Trina rolled her eyes. "You getting on a bike looking like that?"

Cartier had thought of changing from out of her dress and stilettos, but just to annoy her mother, she didn't. Looking directly at Head, she said, "You ready?"

"No doubt." Head leaned over and gave Trina a peck on her cheek. "We'll be back in a few."

Cartier let Head walk out in front of her, and then she turned around and said, "Ma, when we get back remember Head is *my* company, not *our* company, so I don't want you all up in our face all night."

"Cartier, it ain't that serious," Trina said, sashaying back into her lonely compound.

Wearing an electric blue silk dress and silver stilettos, Cartier hopped on the back of Head's bike. Head smirked as he passed her the helmet.

"What's up?"

"You're making my dick hard right now, and you ain't even doing shit."

Cartier reached down, and sure enough, his penis was brick-hard. "We could go back inside, and I could help you with that problem."

He swatted her hand away and readjusted his tool.

"Hold on tight. And don't be screaming like a girl. You might mess up my concentration."

Cartier tapped him playfully on his shoulder and then wrapped her arms as tight as she could around his waist.

The drive into the city was surreal. The way the bike hugged the corners as Head leaned into each turn was exhilarating. The night was clear with a slight breeze, and as they rode over the Manhattan Bridge, Cartier hugged his waist even tighter.

Head took Cartier to Little Italy for a massive pasta dinner. His favorite place was Carmine's, adorned with outside tables, umbrellas, and opera music over their sound system. As they were being seated, he said, "Do you recognize that tune?"

Cartier grimaced. Hell no, she didn't recognize that music. She shook her head rapidly and sat down.

"It's Ennio Morricone. It's the theme song from Robert De Niro's movie, *Once Upon a Time in America*."

Cartier listened more closely. "Hey, you're right. I would have never guessed that."

"What type of music do you like?"

"The usual. Rap, R&B, I guess, a little pop, but mostly hardcore rap. I'm into Fabolous, and Jay-Z, of course, but they got this new kid from Harlem named Chopper that's going hard on the mixtapes."

"What about this tune?"

Cartier pursed her lips and shook her head rapidly. "Umm, not my cup of tea."

"That's because you're not listening with your heart."

"Why do you care? I said I don't like it."

Head chuckled as he picked up the menu. After his eyes briefly scanned the wine list, he put the menu back down and folded his hands. "I care because one day I'd like my wife to walk down the aisle to this."

That information stunned Cartier. "Why would you want your wife to walk down the aisle to a gangster's theme song? And it sounds gloomy, if you ask me."

"Just listen."

"I am listening. 'Here and Now' by Luther Vandross is a little too common for you."

"If you listen with your heart, you'll see it's not gloomy at all. The melody is filled with hope, and so was the film. Robert Deniro's character loved one girl, and only one girl, his whole life. The flute playing throughout represents his loyalty toward that girl and his friends. And even though those closest to him betrayed him, he still remained a consummate friend. That's what I want my wife to feel about me, an undying love, so if even if those around us betray us, the love we have for each other will never die."

Cartier thought about the movie and what it represented to her, and then suddenly she could see his point. And the haunting melody did become a beautiful song. She closed her eyes and took in the whole experience.

"I see what you're saying." Cartier began to get into the next few songs as they ordered dinner.

Finally Head got down to the basics. "I found dude."

"Who? Ryan?"

Head nodded.

"Is he dead?"

"Not yet. I'ma go and handle him tomorrow. My li'l man said every Thursday night he rolls through this gambling joint on 145th Street in Harlem. Niggas go in there around ten, eleven at night and don't come out until daybreak. Everyone coming out that bitch is on high alert, thinking they gonna get juxed 'cause they handling bundles of dough. So I plan to follow him home and get the drop on him and his chick."

Cartier couldn't believe that Head was able to pull off in a couple of weeks what Jason couldn't do in over a year.

"Who's your li'l man?"

"This kid named Leroy."

"Leroy? How long have you known him and are you sure you can trust him. I don't want you walking into a trap."

"Nah, he good peoples. We go way back."

"Well anytime a parent names their child Hank, Earl, Bubba, Leroy or Tyrone—there's gonna be a problem. Those mutherfuckas aren't to be trusted," Cartier joked.

Head laughed, "I can trust him, trust me."

"Are you sure you wanna do this? I mean, you don't really know me. Why would you risk your life, livelihood for me?"

"I thought you'd want to do the same for me. I thought we were on the same page here."

"What do you mean?"

"I mean, we've been talking about starting a new life together—"

"We are."

"Then how am I going to represent to the world that you're my girl, and you got niggas gunning for you? And even if I did decide to chill, once we make it known that you're under my wing, niggas gonna add me to the list."

"But what if they don't? What if they only care about getting at me and Jason?"

All of a sudden Cartier felt uneasy with Head taking over. It was all happening so fast. She didn't think he'd get information on Ryan so quickly, especially since Jason and nosy Bam couldn't.

"I just don't want you getting hurt. I don't know what I'd do if something happened to you. This Ryan don't give a fuck about no one. I told you how he came out of the club blazing." The shootout at Club Roxy flooded Cartier's memory. "I think I should step up to the plate and handle mines."

"Look, Cartier, I ain't no killer, but I've killed. It's how you survive out here. I know how to handle mines, and as I've tried to drill into your thick skull, I don't want you to have no parts of this. Tomorrow, I'ma come and swoop up your family and take all y'all to my crib to lay low until all scores are settled."

What did he just say? Cartier had to fight back tears. She wasn't a punk and wasn't about to cry openly in public. "Well, at least give me the address, so I could give it to Jason. Let's see what he does with the information."

Head pushed his chair back, making a screeching sound. "Are you fucking kidding me?"

Cartier's eyes popped open like that of a child. "What now?"

"You still sweet on that nigga?"

"What? I am not!"

"You still investing in his abilities to handle Ryan, even after all he's done. YOU told me he fucked Jalissa, instead of deading Ryan. YOU told me he forced your hand to pull the trigger. YOU told me the nigga was so grimy, he fucked your homegirl. Now you're going to sit up in my face and tell me to trust dude with my info?"

Cartier couldn't argue with those facts, but she did want to set one thing straight. "The last thing I could give is a fuck about Jason."

Head peered into her eyes, challenging her to look away and show any signs of lying. "Then you won't have a problem with me completing what you started."

Cartier needed to choose her words carefully. "That's only if he still has a vendetta against me, and as it seems, we've both decided to squash the beef."

"You did, huh?"

"Yeah, this morning."

"Word?" It was Head's turn to pop his eyes open in surprise. "How that happen?"

"Well, I went to see him."

Head shifted in his chair, causing Cartier to pause.

Then she continued. "I went to see him to give him back his car. I told him we were together, that I didn't want anything of his, including his car and house. So the kids and I will be homeless." Cartier had to throw the lie on thick. She realized Head had a jealous streak. She hated to admit it, but it made her feel secure in their relationship. It was silly, but his anger made her know, if she wasn't the only girl he was fucking with as he'd told her, she was the one he was most feeling.

"See, that's what I'm saying. Fuck that nigga! He ain't shit." Head leaned forward in his chair. "How he gonna kick out you and his kids on the streets? That's not what real niggas do."

"So I should stay in the house?"

"Hell no! I got you and your family. I'm saying, he shouldn't have made you leave; that should have been your choice. Anyway, Jason got that young money. I'ma show you how a nigga with grown-man money will treat you."

Cartier showed her pearly whites. "Really?"

"Really, ma."

"OK, then it's settled. I don't want to discuss this too much more, but just so that we're clear, I'm going to move out of Jason's house, and you're not going to touch him, right? For the sake of our kids, I don't want him touched."

Head couldn't believe her hypocrisy. It was all right for her to fill him with bullets, but for him, Jason was off limits? "

Cartier, what's changed between you and him?"

"I just told you. Nothing. I swear on everything I love, nothing's changed. We're done. Now promise me you won't do anything to him."

"I can't promise you, because I keep all my promises."

"But he doesn't have a beef with you. I told him about you, and he's cool with us being together."

"First off, I don't need his permission. And, second, you won't know a nigga got beef with you until the bullet has already left the chamber and is lodged snugly in your temple."

"Head, I've seen Jason. He's all fucked up. He can't hurt a fly."

The waitress came and took their orders, providing a much-needed distraction for Cartier.

"Look, let me enjoy my meal," Head said. "We'll kick it about this later."

❧

After dinner, Head decided to take Cartier to where he rested his head at night, a large apartment in the cut of Brighton Beach, a predominantly Russian-Jewish community.

Cartier used to think you couldn't pay a Black person to live there, but obviously she was wrong. "How did they let you in here?" she wondered out loud.

"Money affords you everything."

"I didn't mean it like that. This isn't exactly the lap of luxury. I meant, aren't they usually racist, only letting in their own kind?"

"I know exactly what you meant. As I said, money will afford you anything. I mean"—Head kicked off his Air Nike—"I know this isn't the Taj Mahal, but it's a temporary joint until you go house-hunting for us."

"I thought you'd live in some grand mansion."

"I knew that's what you thought. After I got out the prison, I found this little hideout, until I figured out what I wanted to do. I had lost touch with so many people and wasn't ready to relocate until I had rubbed shoulders with all that I loved. Family, friends, you know, get all that out of my system."

"This place is immaculate. Are you this neat, or do you have a housekeeper? Some Russian chick in a maid's outfit dusting not only your furniture, but your dick as well?"

Head laughed. "I do like the whole maid thing. Maybe we could get you one so you could dust my dick all day. But I'm only into my sistas."

Cartier walked farther into his apartment in her stiletto heels, dress draping over all her curves, and her butt jiggling with every step. She knew he was watching her intensely.

"After you finish taking your tour, call your moms and your kids and tell her that you're safe with me and that you won't be coming home tonight. No need to have her worrying."

Cartier did a salute. "Yes, bossman."

Cartier walked around the spacious but humble three-bedroom apartment with the old-school hardwood floors that would give you a splinter, a standard eat-in kitchen with white appliances, not to mention a king-size bed, large LED television, Wii station, and about one hundred sneaker boxes stacked from floor to ceiling.

As Cartier made herself comfortable on his plush

mattress, she toyed with the idea of letting him know that she was going to meet Jason tomorrow at Trina's, but she decided against it. Shortly thereafter, Head walked in with a pint of Häagen-Dazs vanilla ice cream and two spoons.

"You trying to get me fat?"

"Only with my baby."

"A baby?"

"First comes love, then marriage, then a baby." He kissed her forehead. "You wouldn't want a little me?"

"You don't think it's a little too soon to be putting all of this on our shoulders?"

Head shoved a large scoop into her mouth to shut her up. "Cartier, I know what I want. I'm a go-getter. Always have been, and always will be. If there's one thing my past has taught me is that you gotta live your best life now. You don't get a second chance. I'm thirty-six years old, never been married, and I don't have no kids. When I got locked up, it hurt me that I'd never been a father. I'd never have a wedding, a real wedding with the wife of my choice, not that jailhouse shit with some random chick coming to see her cousin or brother. Now that I'm out and I beat that case, I'm moving at the speed of lightning. So if you're not in love with me yet, then you better hurry up and fall, because I don't have time to make this a long, drawn-out courtship. And because I've already fallen in love with you so, you better catch up."

Cartier didn't reply. She didn't know what to say. Instead, she put down the ice cream and made love to him all night long.

CHAPTER 26

Frienemies

Every night Marisol would wake up in a cold sweat, clutching her chest from pain and screaming out in a blood-curdling moan, visions of Jalissa's badly beaten body with dime-sized bullet holes indelibly etched in her memory. The guilt of not only being the one to encourage Jalissa to hook up with Jason so they could milk him for his money, and then also missing her chance to murder Cartier when she'd spotted her driving down the boulevard was palpable. Marisol should have known that Jalissa was no match for Cartier.

She picked up the untraceable mobile phone and dialed her informant. "Yo, I already told you what will happen to you if you don't get me close to this bitch!" she screamed into the phone. "Now where the fuck does she live?"

"I don't know yet. She never gave us her address."

"So get it!"

"If I ask for it now, then she'll know something is up," the girl whined. "She's not stupid. If she knows I've switched sides, she'll kill me."

"And what the fuck do you think I'll do to you?"

"Look, you can stop with all these threats! I want her dead too! I told you, if you just chill, I would do it myself."

"No! She's mine. Besides, if you had the balls to do it, you wouldn't have contacted me."

"I contacted you because I wanted the bounty you put on her and Jason's heads. Is it still fifty thousand a head?"

Marisol tossed her eyes toward the sky. There wasn't any way the informant would see a dime of that money. "Yes, it's still the same, but I'm going to raise the stakes. If you could get the information for me to get at her before this week ends, then I'll double it. I can't sleep at night with her still walking this earth while my sister's body is rotting in a lonely grave."

"What about Jason? Do you still want him?"

"Of course, I do!"

"And how are you going to get all that cash? Is Ryan going to give it to you?"

The greedy bitch was irking Marisol's nerves, but she knew she had to rein in her anger to get the end result. "It was his idea to up the ante. He's already given me that gwap."

"Good. Because you can get them both, this evening. They're going to be on our block at her mother's apartment." The informant laughed. "We're supposed to sit at the round table and plot you and Ryan's murder."

CHAPTER 27

Playing With Fire

"Good morning," Cartier said sweetly into her cell, turning over on Head's plush mattress. He'd gone to take a shower, so this was an opportunity for her to speak with her mother frankly.

"Good morning?" Trina's voice elevated in surprise. "Since when you start using manners? You must be putting on airs in front of that nigga. Where he at? He laying right next to you?"

"Ain't nobody putting on. Damn!"

Trina snorted, still a little miffed at the way Cartier had carried on with her the night before in front of Head. And when she thought about them not coming back to the house as he'd promised, leaving her to babysit, she got even more angry.

"What time are you coming home? Because I gave birth to three kids, not five. I'm not going to keep being your live-in nanny. You're not Angelina Jolie."

Cartier chuckled. She knew her mother was trying to pick a fight, but she wasn't going to buy in to it. "Now what does Angelina have to do with anything?"

"You must think you're some sort of celebrity, with the hours you keeping, running in and out of here with no care in the world."

"Ma, I have cares, and I have worries, but I can't spend every waking moment riding up and down the streets of New York looking for Ryan with a pistol in the palm of my hand. I already told you that I'm on high alert, watching my back and trying to settle the score. Can't I have one day here and there to keep me from going insane? You have your soap operas, and now I have Head. Why do you keep trying to ruin this?"

Trina acquiesced. "Well, the kids are fine, and I'm fine too. You don't have to rush home."

"Thanks, Ma. I only have a few minutes before Head gets out of the shower. I need your help."

If there was one thing that would always remain unchanged was Trina's loyalty to her daughter. The moment Cartier said she needed help, Trina's attitude shifted from the being a bickering nag to the protective mother. "What happened?"

"Remember, we were all supposed to meet up in Brooklyn tonight with Jason to discuss stepping up our efforts to get at Ryan and Marisol?"

"Yeah. So?"

"So I can't make the meeting. I'm not going to cancel it, because Jason might have some valuable information. Let everyone meet there, and keep telling them I'm coming. I'll need you to head up the meeting and ask all the questions I would. Meanwhile, Head wants me to go home and grab a few of our things and move us into his place."

"When you say us, I hope you just mean you, not me and the kids, right?"

"He means all of us. That means the kids and you too."

"What? Why, Cartier? I'm comfortable here."

"Ma, it's only temporary."

"Well, how does his place feel to you? Is it safe?"

"Safe? Of course, it feels safe. It's definitely on the low, and he hasn't ever invited anyone over. Do you think I would bring the children here if it wasn't safe?"

Trina was still reluctant. "No one knows about this place either, except Jason. And you said yourself he'd never do anything to hurt his kids. With the alarm system, surveillance cameras, and iron French doors, I'm not saying it's Fort Knox, but it's the closest thing to it."

"Well, as I said, it's only temporary, and honestly, Ma, he's promised that he will outshine the house Jason bought us. But I really don't care about all of that. I mean, it did make me smile, but I can buy our own house. It made me happy inside because he wants to do it. You feel me? And I want him to *want* to do it. I'm not saying I need a man. I don't. But I want one. I want Head. It feels good waking up to him each morning. I don't know about you, but I don't want to grow old alone."

Trina knew what Cartier was trying to say. Cartier had always been independent. When Trina wasn't stepping up to the plate as a mother, she went out there and made her own moves.

"Why are you doing all of this cloak-and-dagger stuff?"

"Ma, there isn't any way I'm going to tell Head that I'm meeting with Jason tonight, nor is there any way I'm calling off this meeting. Jason might have valuable information."

"But I thought you said Head is going to handle this?"

"He is." Cartier exhaled, frustrated by her mother's intense line of questioning. "But I'm not going to put all my eggs in one basket. Head got a locale on where Ryan gambles once a week. What if he doesn't show up tonight? Then that means we gotta wait another week? Nah, not when bullets are flying through my window. We need as many people active on this as possible. So, for the meantime, I have to keep Head and Jason as far apart as possible. I have a feeling if Head finds out that I'm still communicating with Jason about Ryan, or if I came out to meet up with Jason tonight, then I feel Head will certainly pull away."

"Why don't you tell him that he ain't got anything to worry about? That you and Jason are done?"

"That's all I've been telling him, but he doesn't believe me. He knows that, not only am I Jason's wife, but I have his kids. I know Head says he ain't the jealous type, but he had someone he loved leave him, and if I were him, I'd be just a little cautious about dating a married chick. I just want to keep his worries at a minimum until we have more time under our belts and I get those divorce papers."

"OK, so I'ma give you my truck to run home and pack up your family, and also this spare key." Head tossed Cartier both sets. "I'll meet you back here around seven to meet your little ones and get everyone settled, and then I'll head back out to handle dude."

It was already after four o'clock when Cartier headed back out toward Long Island. Trina had the kids all packed and ready, and Janet was there to drive Trina back to Brooklyn.

"Remember, make sure y'all drill the fuck out of Jason."

"What makes you think he has any info to drill?" Trina asked.

"That slimy bastard better have some information, if he knows what's good for him," Janet said. "And he better hope I don't put my foot in his trifling ass."

Janet was still pissed off that Jason was sleeping with Jalissa. Everyone was. No one trusted him as far as they could see him. He'd betrayed everyone's trust.

"Well, I know we're all furious with Jason, and I'm not going to try to say that I feel the most betrayed because he's my husband. Janet, I know you're just as hurt because this was, and always has been, about Shanine and Monya. But we need a remedy. And if Jason could finally step up to the plate and give us something—anything— that could help move us forward, then we gotta allow him that. So don't go in there slinging accusations or trying to make him feel guilty about his actions. He won't. Had he had any feelings for anyone beside himself, he would have never hooked up with her to begin with. And also keep in mind how immature he is. If you go down that road, I know him; he'll act like a little child and walk out with his lips poked out without giving up any information."

"And we'll beat the shit out of him. Ain't that right, Janet?" Trina exclaimed.

"Let him try that stupid shit and he won't make it out that front door. I swear 'fore God, I'll stab him!"

"And I'll hold him down."

The two feisty older women thought together they were invincible. Cartier felt nostalgic. That was supposed to be her and Monya in twenty year's time.

"Well, don't agitate him to act reckless. Everyone needs to keep their feelings in check, for the sake of Shanine and Monya, and for my future. These niggas are on my ass, and it's only a matter of time before they get the drop on me, if we don't get the drop on them first."

Cartier met Head back at his apartment as she'd promised, kids in tow. This would be the first time he'd meet her two little sisters, Fendi and Prada, and her children, Christian and Jason Jr.

She was in the kitchen making dinner when he walked in. There was something über sexy about Head to her. His masculinity mixed with his maturity was endearing.

"I see we got a full house," Head said, walking through the door, his warm smile directed toward the four children playing happily in the living room.

They all stopped what they were doing and looked up at the strange man.

"Who are you?" Fendi stood protectively in front of her baby sister, niece, and nephew.

"My name's Henry. A friend of your sister's."

That was the first time Cartier had heard Head's government name. She walked closer and stood within a few feet of Head. "Hey, Christian, Jason, come over here and meet my friend. This is who Mommy has been telling you about."

The kids could care less about the stranger. They wanted to go home. They inched closer to Head with suspicious eyes, drinking him in.

The talkative Christian spoke up first. "Are you my mommy's new boyfriend?"

Head chuckled and looked to Cartier.

"He's a friend of mine, Christian. Now say hello, and go finish playing."

"Are we gonna live here with you?"

"We're going to hang out here for a few days."

"But we don't like it here."

"OK, that's enough. Go back and play until I fix dinner. Head, you wanna come in here with me?"

"Nah, I think I'll stay out here and get to know my guests a little better." He sat down on the sofa. "What are y'all playing?"

Prada said, "We wanna play with your game, but Cartier said no."

Head looked at Cartier like she was the wicked witch.

"Of course you can play with my game. Here, let me turn it on for you."

Cartier walked back into the kitchen and continued to fix dinner. Shortly thereafter, Head walked in and began to help her by dicing up the vegetables.

"What you got going on in here?"

"Well, you had steak and more steak in your freezer, so I thought I'd cook steak." Cartier laughed.

"Not a bad choice." Head leaned over and gave her a kiss. "Listen, after I eat I'm going to bounce out of here and go handle that. Don't expect me back home until early tomorrow morning."

Cartier inhaled her fears. She hoped that by this time tomorrow evening Ryan and Marisol would have gone to meet their Maker. That Head would be safe.

As if reading her mind, Head said, "And don't spend all evening worrying about me. I'll be fine. On that I'll make a promise."

Cartier wanted to think only positively, but her gut kept telling her that she couldn't rest easy until Head walked back through the door.

"Oh, I forgot to ask. Where's Trina?"

Cartier fumbled and wiped her hands on the dishrag. "She decided to stay the night at Janet's. Honestly, she wasn't too keen about moving in here with us, but I'm sure she'll be here tomorrow."

"I can feel that. If I were in her shoes, I wouldn't want to bounce either. Jason had y'all set up nicely over there. Did you tell her I'm going to top what he did for y'all?"

Cartier shook her head. "It's not that. I mean, my mom knows that at the end of the day she doesn't ever have to worry about who's going to put food on the table. Man or no man, I'll always grind to provide for my family. Her main concern is safety. She wants to know that her family is safe."

"And what did you tell her?"

"I told her what I felt in my heart."

"Which is?"

"That I *could* trust you. That I *do* trust you. And that with you we're safe."

Trina called, and called, but Cartier refused to answer while Head was still home. As soon as he left, her fingers couldn't dial her mother fast enough. She needed to hear what information Jason had to offer.

"Did he have any details about Ryan and Marisol?"

"You know, that slimy bastard never showed up."

"What?" Cartier's heart sank. Inwardly she was hoping Jason would redeem himself. Somehow she felt he knew more about Ryan and Marisol than he was letting on, and that if he gave them up, then it would be like she'd won—that he did love her more than he'd loved Jalissa.

"How he gonna not show up?"

"How should I know?"

"Well, did he at least call?"

"Hell no! He had all of us waiting here for hours, stuck on stupid."

"That nigga continually disappoints me," Cartier said. "Well, thank goodness, I still got Head. He's out there now trying to take care of my problem."

"OK, well, I've decided to stay here in Brooklyn at my apartment. With Jason out there going rogue, I'll feel much safer here. Come through in the morning."

"Will do."

❧

The knife being plunged into Jason's thigh wasn't enough for him to give them what they wanted. And even when the knife was twisted, causing him to scream out in mind-numbing pain, his heart still couldn't give in.

"Look, Jason, me and you don't got no beef. This could all end tonight if you tell me where I can find Cartier and that new nigga she fucking."

"Man, fuck that! Just do you and get this over with!"

At first Jason thought Cartier had set him up. He'd left the rehabilitation center as he said he would and headed over to Trina's. He hadn't even put his car fully in park when the gun was jammed into his back and he was tossed into the backseat. Twenty-four hours later he was delirious, dehydrated, and certain of two things—Cartier didn't set him up, and he wasn't walking out of there alive.

"It don't got to be this way," Ryan said, circling Jason, who was duct-taped to a wooden chair. "I know you only stepped in to get at me to impress your wife. I know how women are." He looked toward Marisol. "They can be really persuasive when they need to be. I know if it were up to you, you'd be out fucking a brand-new chick every night and concentrating on getting that paper. Look, I'm ready to wave the white flag if you give me what I need. You can get a pass, and go and raise your kids in peace, but your wife—whether you help us or not—is dead. She sealed her fate when she killed Jalissa."

Marisol hauled off and punched Jason in his right jaw with such force, his neck almost snapped. She pushed the knife that was already lodged into his thigh farther down. Jason screamed a guttural moan, but they were confident no one would hear him. They were in the basement of a local bodega that Ryan owned in Sunset Park, Brooklyn as a front to launder his drug money.

"Shut up!" Marisol yelled. She dug her sharp nails deep into his face and pulled.

Jason, feeling like his face was split open, launched a mouthful of phlegm into her porcelain skin. The gooey liquid startled Marisol, who stepped back out of his space and blinked her eyes rapidly in horror.

Ryan shook his head. "That was a bad move, bro."

"Man, fuck y'all muthafuckas! I ain't giving y'all shit on my wife, so however you gotta get your hands dirty, just get it over with! All this Colombo bullshit is wack."

After sitting in a cold, damp basement overnight without any food or water, Jason knew he was at the end of his rope. No pleading or bitching up was going to save him. He'd never thought he'd be on the receiving end of an ambush. Not on the block that he'd grown up on and trusted in broad daylight. He realized, too late, how much heart Ryan truly had. At any second, Wonderful, Blake, Cartier, or The Cartel could have pulled up, and the mere sight of Ryan would have initiated a bloodbath.

Jason knew Cartier always doubted whether or not he truly loved her, but facing death, there wasn't any doubt in his heart that he loved her more than his actions could have ever shown, or words could have ever conveyed. Jalissa was just one of many phases he'd gone through. No different than Monya or Mari. He would have tired of her eventually, but he never got the chance. He would have accepted her as one of his baby mommas and moved on.

Cartier was where his heart lay. She was his one true love. He knew he wasn't capable of being faithful and could do some downright grimy things. Foolishly he thought his good actions, holding Cartier down and marrying her while she was locked up, buying her a house, whip, things like that, proved his loved and would outweigh the dumb shit he did. He had that archaic way of thinking, which was that all men cheated, married or not. And he was just fucking those side chicks but would ultimately get right back to making Cartier happy after he got his cheating ways out of his system.

Being tortured couldn't break his loyalty to Cartier, not even after she'd tried to kill him, because he understood her actions. She loved him so much, she couldn't bear sharing him with anybody else. He realized that when Wonderful told him about Cartier and Head. A part of him broke inside, and he was filled with a blind rage, where it was his mission to kill Head.

Jason truly believed Cartier was a good wife, that she loved him. He knew he would never get to tell her how he really felt and could only hope she would keep his memory alive for their kids. And at this moment, he even hoped that she and Head truly had something because, although Cartier got busy, anyone could get caught slipping. And Cartier would need all the soldiers she could get on her team because, as it stood now, Ryan and Marisol were definitely not going to rest until she was dead.

Marisol walked over to the flimsy foldaway table that was littered with torture tools—a wrench, knives, pliers, an extension cord, flex cuffs, and a taser gun. The five thousand volts being blasted into his body felt like bolts of lightning. Jason's body began to convulse, and then it stiffened. Then his head lolled to one side, and he whimpered softly.

With spit drooling from his mouth, and hot urine dripping down his left leg, Jason could feel his body shutting down.

"Damn, man!" Ryan jeered. "I should make your ass clean this shit up!"

"R-R-Ryan, promise me that you won't hurt Cartier. She's been through enough. You ain't gotta take it that far. We street, nigga." Jason paused to gather strength. "Once I'm gone, she'll fold. I promise you that."

Ryan was hoping that all this torture would get the need to seek blood out of Marisol's system. He needed her to feel he was doing everything he could in his power to get at Cartier. One part of him knew Jason was a street dude and there wasn't any way he'd give up Cartier. If niggas got you tied up in a room, they ain't letting you go. So Ryan was confident that Jason wouldn't fall for his proposition. But even if Jason did give up the location on Cartier, Ryan new that Head had pulled her out of that crib, so either way, he had covered all the bases. If Jason gave up an address before they killed him, he'd take Marisol there in his final attempt to pretend to be looking to catch Cartier.

Jason pleading for Ryan to spare Cartier set Marisol off. Who the fuck was this bitch that these niggas kept protecting? Deep down inside she felt that Ryan could have deaded Cartier. Why did he keep hesitating? Did he still love her? Was there something special about her that had these men pledging their allegiance?

"Ryan don't give a fuck about your whore, bitch-wife! And Jalissa never gave a fuck about you! She was using your gullible ass, and look where it got you!"

Jason's voice was barely a whisper. "No, look where it got her." He was perspiring heavily, and the room was now drenched with urine, sweat, and fear.

Marisol decided that there wasn't any way she'd be kind and put a bullet in his dome. That would be too nice. She picked up the Anderson all-metal baseball bat and held it snugly in between her manicured fingertips.

"Ryan, before I end this, you want to tell him who set him up and let us know about the meeting tonight?" Marisol asked.

"Nah, let him go out wondering."

"W-W-Wait," Jason began. This news had piqued his interest. The words *set up* caught him off guard. "T-T-Tell me what you know."

❧

Cartier awoke the next morning without Head in bed lying next to her. Immediately, she began to worry. Her heart was fluttering as she dialed his cell phone, which just rang out.

He's OK, she thought to herself. *Nothing's happened.*

All morning she continually hit redial. She couldn't count the number of messages she'd left. Not one to be too emotional, Cartier found herself crying her eyes out, which she thought silly, because she hadn't heard any news, good or bad.

"Trina, Head didn't come home last night," she said, her voice laced with concern.

"Oh, dear God! Do you think they got the drop on him?"

"I don't know what to think. I'm so confused."

"And you've tried his cell phone?"

"Of course. I keep leaving messages, but he's not returning any of my calls."

"OK. I want you to get out of there now and come over here until he calls you. You don't know what's up."

"Do you think he's dead?"

"Cartier, don't ask questions I can't answer. Just scoop up the kids and get over here. I'm not going to feel at ease until you're in my sight. And, Cartier?"

"Yes?"

"Make sure you're strapped, and be careful loading the kids into the cars. Any sign of danger, start bucking shots first. No questions need to be asked."

"OK, I hear you."

They hung up the phone, and two seconds later Trina called her back.

"You know what? Give me the address to Head's house. Janet and I will come and get you. I can't risk you bringing four kids alone. I don't like the way this is going down. First, no Jason last night, and then no Head. Jason could have something to do with Head not coming home, and if that's true, then he'll be gunning for you next."

∽

Cartier sat tight until Trina and Janet arrived. Both ladies were strapped as they squeezed everyone into Janet's car.

"Damn, this is getting way out of control. This beef thing keeps expanding, Cartier. I sure hope and pray that Head is all right."

Once again Cartier began to cry, her heavy tears almost blinding her until they arrived into Brooklyn.

"Isn't that Jason's wheels?" Janet remarked dryly.

Everyone in the car peered out the window to see the distinctive white Benz with H8TER plates parked a few houses away from Trina's apartment.

"Yeah, Cartier gave it back to him a couple days ago, but what's it doing parked on this block? He must have just arrived. Do you think he thought the meeting was today?" Trina replied.

Cartier remained quiet. Head's absence weighing heavy on her.

"Why you did that? That nigga wouldn't have gotten shit back from me. I'd burn it to the ground before he'd ever see that car again." Janet was in rare form.

Finally, Cartier broke her silence. "I gave it back because it's his."

"All he gonna do is have some bitch riding shotgun," Trina said.

"I don't care, Ma. I'm with Head now."

"Sometimes I think, when it comes to a nigga, you go soft. Let that had been a chick who disrespected you, you would have ripped that car to pieces with your bare hands."

"Ain't nobody going soft over no nigga. It's his car, Ma. That's the only thing he's getting. He also wanted the house, and I told him to beat it."

Trina remained silent, so Cartier could grasp how stupid she sounded, a tactic that worked.

Cartier began to doubt her decision. "So I shouldn't have given him the car?"

"That's what I said."

"Pull over," Cartier demanded. "Let's lay low on him to see who he's fucking with."

"You can't be serious."

"What?"

"You still on that nigga dick!" Trina said, disgusted.

"Why the hell do you care? Didn't he already show you what's really good?"

Trina's harsh words knocked Cartier upside her head. She was playing herself. "Well, still pull over. I got a trick for his ass."

Reluctantly Janet pulled over and hopped out.

With the spare set of keys, Cartier stole Jason's car. "Follow me," she said, grinning from ear to ear.

Trina and Janet weren't amused. Both women felt she should have never given back the car; destroying it would have been better.

"Jason is gonna flip when he comes out and see his ride gone. He gonna swear someone stole his shit," Janet stated.

"You know you better park that ride because within a few hours the cops will be looking for it."

"So let them look. Ma, it's in your name."

"But you're not me, Cartier. Also, you ride dirty all the time. Do you really want to take the chance that they take you into custody for this bullshit Benz and find out you got a gun on you? That's mandatory three years for you, with your record. Cartier, it's just not worth it."

"I guess you're right. I'll park it for now. If he gives up some information, then he could have it back. If he doesn't, then I'm gonna pay a crackhead to burn it to the ground. Follow me on Miller Avenue, and then let's head back to Trina's to see if he's waiting around for us to tell us some information that we need to hear. I told him that this shit needs to come to a head."

As Janet pulled over, her mouth was going a mile a minute. "Speaking of Head, how does he feel about this? And since when you and Jason on speaking terms? And when did his cripple ass get out of the clinic?"

Cartier laughed. "I told you that he doesn't officially sign out until next week, but he was coming out so everyone could strategize about those losers. I told him what happened to me the other day when they shot up my car, and he went beserk. I was so scared that he might injure himself even more than he already was."

Janet sucked her teeth. "Two tears in a bucket."

Back at Janet's, Cartier called Li'l Momma and Bam to come over. Tension was flying and Cartier was almost frantic that she couldn't get in touch with Head. As everyone sat down, Cartier could feel uneasiness in the room, but she didn't know where it was coming from.

"Why your face all twisted up?" she asked Li'l Momma, although, had she put up a mirror in front of Bam's face, both would have been identical.

"Look, I'ma keep it real with you and say my piece. I'd appreciate if you keep it real in return."

"A'ight, kick it."

"I had a bad taste in my mouth for some time about how you handled me and Bam, regarding your residence. The moment you moved out of the hood, Bam and I got rearranged. We were no longer like sisters. You treated us like distant cousins by keeping your address away from us. I know in the hood, when you have beef, you have to watch those closest to you, but I never thought you'd carry me and Bam like that."

"I hear you, and you're right. Jason was around, and he was making all the rules, but there's no excuse. I should have put my foot down, but I didn't. I guess I was a little scared for the kids, not of you and Bam, but not wanting to start an argument, I gave in. Honestly Li'l Momma, I didn't want Wonderful or Blake to know where we lived. You know I trust you and Bam with my life, but you know how niggas do. They ride for their niggas. You see what happened with Tarsha and Drac from Cypress. His best friend set him up and killed them both, put a bullet in the back of both their heads while she was six months pregnant. And what about Breezy and Jinx from Bed Stuy? Her own friend stabbed her numerous times for that paper."

Li'l Momma shook her head. "I understand somewhat, but still . . ."

"I know. And I promise you that from here on out, no secrets. I don't give a fuck who I'm with. Cool?"

"Cool. A'ight, so now tell me what's up with Head and Jason."

"Whew!" Cartier exhaled. "Jason is being officially released any day now. But hopefully today he's coming through to spill his guts about Jalissa and find out if he has any clues that could lead us to Ryan and Marisol. And as far as Head, he left last night seeing what info he could find on Ryan. He doesn't want me in this beef no more, so he has no idea I'm even meeting up with y'all, or Jason for that matter. He keeps talking about making an honest woman out of me, and to him that means no more toting guns, moving weight, fighting, or killing. And he wants to marry me."

"Does he know you're already married?" Li'l Momma raised her eyebrow quizzically.

"How could he not know? Didn't you drop dime?"

"Oh, my bad."

"He wants me to get a divorce." Cartier stared directly into Li'l Momma's eyes. Just talking about Head and not knowing where he was kept eating away at her.

"What do you want?"

Cartier blushed, thinking about the possibilities. "I want that too."

After a full hour of getting nothing accomplished, Cartier's focus returned to Head, who she'd still not heard from. She sat wringing her hands, pacing up and down the apartment. Trina tried to tell her he was all right, but she wasn't buying it. And to make matters worse, she couldn't get in touch with Jason.

"I'm ordering Chinese food. Do you want anything?"

"Nah, I'm good," Cartier replied.

Cartier took a moment to put together her next move. *What if they're both dead?* A slight chill ran down her spine. *What if Ryan got the drop on both men in her life? Could he be that crafty?* Cartier was definitely on edge. She continually dialed each phone, but both were going straight to voicemail.

That morning, after a long, sleepless night, Cartier woke up to take all kids to school, but not before calling Li'l Momma.

"Suit up. I have to take Christian to the doctor in an hour. After I drop her back off, we're going uptown to handle Ryan's moms."

"What do you mean when you say *handle*?"

"She gotta go! That's the only way—"

"What the fuck are you talking about? We don't go around killing people's moms just because you say so! Certain things are off limits. We hit his mom, and then he'll hit yours, or mines!"

"You don't understand. My hands are tied."

"Cartier, I understand perfectly. You've lost your mind. Nothing is worth having his mother's blood on your hands. It's not gonna bring back Shanine or Monya. If you go ahead with this, you're on your own. And that's hard for me to say."

"It ain't that hard, 'cause you just said it."

"You're bugging. Yesterday you gave a whole song and dance about Head wanting you out the game and handling this. What happened to that? That nigga done bailed?"

Cartier sucked her teeth. "Unlike other muthafuckas in my life, he ain't bail on me." She choked back tears. "I think he's dead."

"Dead? Why you think that?"

"I just have a strong feeling in my stomach that something has happened to him and Jason. I haven't heard from either one of them in over twenty-four hours."

Li'l Momma said, "So they're not returning your calls?"

"At all. And now both phones are going straight to voicemail."

Li'l Momma's two-way line clicked. "Cartier, that's Bam. Let me fill her in on what's going on. Take the kids to school, and Cee Cee to the doctor, and then we'll meet you back at Trina's."

"Thanks, sis."

CHAPTER 28

Usual Suspects

Cartier felt too antsy waiting around an hour before she had to take Christian to the doctor's office. She called to see if they could squeeze her in earlier, and they could. Swooping up her baby girl, she jumped in Jason's ride and aimlessly went straight to pick up Bam to see if she would ride with her.

"What are you doing here?"

"Ride with me to take Christian to the doctor's."

"But I thought you weren't leaving for another hour."

"I wasn't, but shit changed. Did Li'l Momma tell you about Head and Jay?"

"You know it."

"So, grab your purse so we could kick it. Mentally, I feel like I'm losing it."

Bam hesitated momentarily, but when she saw the desperation in Cartier's eyes, she grabbed her keys, and they were gone.

The appointment went by quickly, and before Cartier could fully understand what was happening, she'd dropped off Christian with Trina, and she and Bam were on their way to pick up Li'l Momma.

Once in the car, Li'l Momma made herself comfortable. "So, I take it, no word from Jason or Head?"

Cartier's eyes welled up. "Nothing. I'm telling you they're both dead."

"Cartier, stop saying that until you know for sure," Bam said. "You could be jinxing them."

"Then where are they?"

"We can't answer that, and you know it," Li'l Momma said softly.

The whole car remained silent.

Li'l Momma continued, "Where are we going?"

"Hear me out, first. We're not going to do anything, but I want to ride uptown and just perch close to his mom's house. What if by chance he shows up? That's all I wanna do. Just watch her crib."

Both friends could hear her desperation. Cartier's next outburst shocked everyone. She began sobbing her heart out. "I can't keep living like this! This shit is taking too long." She pounded on the steering wheel to drill home her point. "This nigga done killed everyone I love, and I can't touch him? People get murdered in the hood every day. Why not Ryan? This is like some boring movie! Just drawn out for no reason!"

More tears, and then accusations began flying.

"And, Bam, what good are you? It's been how long and you can't get any information on Ryan?"

Bam wanted to say a few scathing remarks but decided against it. Cartier was just venting.

"Since day one I'm always the only one to step up to the plate and get things handled. But what are you and Li'l Momma really good for? Find me Ryan!" The last sentence came out in a screechy pitch as Cartier drove at a reckless speed over the FDR Drive.

Bam and Li'l Momma buckled up and silently prayed that their car wouldn't be wrapped around a pole.

Shortly thereafter, Cartier began to calm down. Her breathing returned back to normal, and she wiped her anguish away. When she pulled at a safe distance on Ryan's mother's block, she turned off the ignition, and they all began the waiting game.

Four hours later, no one had said a word, taken a bathroom break, or had anything to eat.

When Cartier's phone began ringing, her heart inflated with hope. *Could this be Head? Or Jason?* She couldn't answer the phone quickly enough. "Hello?" she breathed anxiously into the phone.

"Yo, C, we gotta kick it."

"Who's this?"

"This is Wonderful. Where you at?"

Cartier hesitated. Why was Wonderful calling her? It had to do with Jason, she was sure. "I'm around." She didn't feel she could trust him with the information that she was laying low on Ryan.

"Are you alone?"

It wasn't what he'd said, but how he'd said it. Instinctively Cartier tossed up her index finger, letting Bam and Li'l Momma know she'd be right back, and hopped out of the car. She knew this was a risky, life-threatening move, so she put her head down low, hunched her shoulders, and began walking.

Four blocks later, she sat down on a stoop and said, "I am now. What's up?"

"It's Jay. I don't think duke is still alive."

Cartier's heart sank. "I have the same feeling. Is he not calling you back either?"

"I spoke to him two days ago about midday. He said he was gonna bounce, to come and meet you, to clear up that Jalissa shit. I told him that me and Blake might not be able to make it because we were driving back from OT on some business, but if we landed back in town, we'd hit him up. He told me what happened while you had the kids in the car. That shit was fucked up—"

"Thanks, Wonderful."

"Anyway, he said after you left, he tried to think of any clues he could that might help, and he remembered a long time ago Jalissa had him drop her off in Sunset Park in Brooklyn. She told him she was going to see her aunt. Jay said he pulled off, only to circle the block. And the same building that she pretended to go in as soon as she thought he'd left, she backpedaled out of that block and proceeded to walk a few blocks down. He said he was going to go back to the area and see if he could find the block, and from there he was going to meet up with you."

"Oh, my gosh! He never made it."

"Well, sort of. He did go back to the area and find the block, and then he called and gave that information to me. He said there was one tenement building and a local bodega. The last call from him I received was that he was only a few blocks from you."

Cartier was getting impatient. She wasn't sure what his point was. "Wonderful, are you saying you think I have something to do with Jason missing?"

"Nah, Ma. I'm saying that I have Jason's murder recorded on my answering machine."

Cartier dropped her phone and almost died. Her hands trembled as she picked back up her cell phone. "Did you just say that Jason is dead?"

Wonderful was still shaken up. "Yeah, it seems so. There isn't any way he'd survive what I just heard."

Cartier was almost frightened to ask. "Who did it? Was it Head?"

"Head?" Wonderful questioned. When she didn't repeat the name, he began to tell her all that he knew. "I'm not sure how it happened . . . if Jay was clever enough to dial my number, or if his phone dialed on its own. But my answering machine can record up to sixty minutes of conversation. It wasn't until now that I had time to listen to my messages and, Cartier . . ."

"What?"

"It was enough to make a hard-core nigga like myself break down and cry. First off, that nigga Ryan and Marisol jammed him up. They tortured him, trying to get your location, but he wouldn't give it up."

Tears began streaming down Cartier's flushed cheeks. This was surreal.

"They had him begging for them to just end it and kill him."

Cartier had to cover her mouth to keep her from screaming out her pain.

Wonderful could hear Cartier sniveling on the other end. "Yo, Cartier, whatever you and Jason went through, that's not my business. No matter what, you're my man's wife, and I know he loved you. But you gotta watch your back. You have a traitor in your crew."

"My crew? What do you mean, I got a traitor in *my* crew? You mean, The Cartel?"

"All I'm doing is repeating what I heard. Before they killed Jason, they asked him if he wanted to know who'd set him up—"

Cartier interjected. "Wonderful, who was it?"

"That's the million-dollar question. My tape ran out at that crucial moment."

Cartier could think of a million reasons one or both of The Cartel members would betray her and Jason. Only, she truly didn't want to. She thought about Ryan. He was probably just taunting Jason.

"Wonderful, for all we know, Ryan could have told Jason that I gave him up. I can't believe that Bam or Li'l Momma could have set Jason up to get killed. Both of them are with me now, laying low to take him out."

Wonderful hesitated for a moment. "As I said, I didn't get a chance to hear a name, but it could be anyone, including me. And what about Janet?"

"Janet?"

"Yeah, Janet. Jason said she's been beefing with him and called him at the rehabilitation center a few times threatening to kill him after she found out he was fucking around with Jalissa. Face it. Anyone could have wanted to see Jason dead. Including Trina."

"Trina? Hold up, Wonderful. First off, we don't know for sure he's dead. And, secondly, why would Trina want him dead?"

"No one will forgive him for fucking with that girl. Not Janet, because her daughter is dead. Trina, because once again, he humiliated her daughter. You, because he wouldn't stop cheating. Bam, for rocking that Mike nigga. Li'l Momma, for Shanine. Weren't they the closest?"

Cartier wondered how Wonderful could break it down like that, but then she remembered that Jason had told him everything, and he'd seen everything from the sideline.

"Wonderful, this is too much to take in. All those people you just named, I would trust with my life."

"Well, you must not value your life much, 'cause a nigga just told you how it went down. You can't trust anyone, or you'll end up like my man."

Cartier wiped her tears. "What's the location of the block?"

"I'ma go with you."

"Nah, I gotta do this one solo. Just like you said, I can't trust no one."

CHAPTER 29

Heartless

Cartier dropped Bam and Li'l Momma back off, not spilling one word of what Wonderful told her. The whole time she kept her eyes peeled from Li'l Momma in the backseat to Bam in the passenger's position. All she kept imagining was either one of them putting a silver bullet in the back of her head. They knew she was upset and had been crying, but she'd told them the telephone call was from Trina, who'd reported she still hadn't heard anything from Head or Jason. She told both girls she was heading over to Head's, but really, she was on a whole other mission.

The night air was extremely brisk for a summer evening. Cartier circled the block numerous times before settling on a hideout. She parked Jason's conspicuous bright white Benz almost a mile away and hiked to the location Wonderful had given her. She had no idea what she was going to do once she got there, nor did she know whether or not she was walking into a trap. All she knew was, those closest to her were dropping like flies.

Clad in oversized jeans and sweat-hood that she'd smeared in dirt, a baseball cap, and kicked up Timberland boots, she pulled her hat low and gripped her gat firmly under her sweatshirt. Cartier trekked toward the location, staggering over to the steps and sitting down. All business establishments were closed—laundromat, cleaners, realtor, and daycare center. The only store open was a bodega that sat in the middle of the block. Cartier sat very closely to the trash bins and pretended to be homeless. She knew that area well, and it was littered with panhandlers, so she'd fit right in.

Cartier sat peering at some young girls walking down the block. They were in five-inch stilettos and dresses so short, if they needed to bend for any reason, they'd be giving a full view of the crack of their asses.

Young gangsters finished their shifts of hugging the block and turned in their hustling clothes for party gear. As the patrons went in and out of the tenement building, no one seemed to care that there was a homeless person just a few feet away.

Minutes turned into hours, and hours felt like days. Cartier wanted to go home and come out to fight another day, but she knew if she wrapped things up tonight, she wouldn't have to come back another day. Besides, the way things were going down, she knew there wouldn't be too many safe days in front of her.

Could someone close to her have really wanted Jason dead? Did someone other than Ryan and Marisol want Cartier dead?

The sharp kick to Cartier's lower back jolted her out of her daydream and thrust her back into reality.

A young thug who was trying to impress his entourage barked at Cartier, "Move ya stink ass off this stoop! This ain't the Holiday Inn!"

The two young girls he was with started giggling.

With her head hanging low, Cartier moved slowly, as an elderly person would, off the stoop and crawled up next to three large garbage cans. As she wrestled the cans to have a seat, a large rat came darting out of its safe haven and skirted across her feet. Cartier stifled a yelp. She knew she needed to control her emotions.

Cartier didn't need to look at her watch to know it was getting late. Fewer cars traveled down the concrete pavements, and the block felt almost desolate. Every thirty minutes or so you'd hear a New York City bus come rumbling down the block to either pick up or drop off a passenger. Still, the bodega remained open. Cartier surmised that it was open twenty-four hours, with one or two customers every hour.

After counting cars, Cartier needed to stretch her legs, cramped from sitting on the cold, hard cement. Bending down to touch her toes, she didn't notice the familiar figure breeze past her. By the time she stood up, he was already gone.

Thirty minutes later, Cartier couldn't believe her eyes when Ryan came walking out of the bodega with a paper bag tucked under his arm and a cell phone glued to his ear.

"I be there in twenty minutes, so keep it warm and wet for daddy," he said.

Cartier's hands began to tremble. She'd pictured this scene over and over in her head for almost a year. She had no idea what she was going to do. She'd always thought The Cartel would kidnap Ryan and torture him to death after he'd confessed to killing Shanine and Monya. She wanted to look directly into his eyes and watch him bitch up as he pleaded for his life. She'd even thought about setting him on fire while he was still alive and watch him scream as his skin melted off his bones.

But in life not everything happens as planned, and in the split second she had before Ryan realized she was walking behind him, she did something unconventional.

"*Whoo-hooo*," she whistled.

Ryan turned around slightly in a non-threatening manner, oblivious to the impending danger. In that split second his mind began racing. Had he done the right thing by setting up Head? He knew that they'd had a truce and that Head was family, but with him out of the way, he wouldn't have to leave New York, which was his territory, and he wasn't about to let anyone run him out.

Ryan tried his hardest to keep his word as a man, but that wasn't his makeup. He'd backstab his own momma, if it would mean advancing.

Now, with a gunman staring him in his face, he wished he'd rethought his decision. Had he kept his promise, he and Marisol would've been looking out on the blue water on Ocean Avenue on the Miami strip, and he'd have his share of Spanish mommies to gawk at. This late-night trip to pick up cash was routine for Ryan. He didn't feel as if he needed a crew, especially since no one was supposed to know about that location.

Before Ryan could reach, Cartier looked him squarely in his eyes, so he could know where the hit came from, and let four hot slugs rip through his body. When he dropped to the ground, she stood over him and pumped three into the back of his head. Oddly enough, she didn't run away. She bent down and picked up his cell phone and could hear the frantic voice of a female.

"You're next, bitch!"

CHAPTER 30

Devil in a New Dress

Of the few people Cartier could trust, Trina was definitely on that list. She and her mother didn't keep any secrets, and if Trina had snitched out Jason, she would have told Cartier.

Cartier tried to creep into the house, to not wake anyone, but Trina was up sitting in the kitchen. The house reeked of cigarette smoke.

"Thank God, you're home." Trina leapt from the table and embraced her daughter as if she'd never see her again. "I have been sitting here all night worrying about you."

"Ma, I'm all right, but first thing tomorrow morning, we gotta bounce."

Trina was ready to get off that block and didn't want to ask too many questions. "OK, cool. I'm ready to go with just the clothes on my back."

Cartier could see that she had her mother worried. She had that same look when the detectives had kicked in the door to arrest Cartier for murder.

"Good, the earlier, the better. I don't know where we're headed just yet. I didn't sort all that out yet. We could probably drive to Jersey and stay at a hotel for a couple weeks until I figure out our next move."

"What happened out there tonight?"

"Ryan is done." Cartier closed her eyes tightly and then opened them to face the reality of the situation. "And I also got his cell phone. I want to give the number to Bam to see if her connect in the telephone company could get an address, but—"

"But what?"

"Wow! Trina, I don't know where to begin. Tomorrow I gotta go to the precinct and file a missing person's report on Jason and Head. I think they're both dead."

"I hate to think like that, but it's been two days."

"Well, not only that." Cartier paused and willed herself to not lose it. "Wonderful called me earlier, and not only did he tell me that Jason called him and his answering machine taped the whole murder—"

"What?"

"Yeah, let me finish. He said that Ryan is caught on tape torturing Jason to give up my location, and from how it sounded, there wasn't any way they left Jason alive. And on top of that info, Ryan also says on the tape that there's a traitor in my camp."

"A traitor? You mean someone is working with Ryan to have you killed? Someone we know?"

"That's what he said, but until I hear the tape for myself, I can't go around accusing anyone. Wonderful even said that Janet could be one of the usual suspects."

Cartier didn't dare tell her mother that he said Trina

too, which would surely have hurt her feelings. She thought Trina would start breaking to take up for Janet, but instead, she just remained silent.

Cartier continued, "So let's break out first thing in the morning without telling anyone. We'll stop by the precinct on our way out, and I'll think of a way of matching an address with the telephone number."

"Well it's always darkest before the dawn, Cartier. You can't give up. You'll find out who's leaking information."

Cartier pulled out Ryan's phone and went through the contacts. Ryan had over two thousand contacts in his iPhone, and when she searched for the obvious names, Li'l Momma, Bam, or Janet, nothing showed up. Then it dawned on her what she'd learned from Mari. If Ryan knew he was dealing with a double agent, he might file the telephone number with a codename.

Cartier' cell phone had to ring six times before it woke her up. It was only seven in the morning, and she'd probably been asleep less than three hours. She'd fallen asleep with Ryan's phone in her hands, going through the massive address book.

"Hello?"

"Babe, finally."

"Head?"

"Yeah, it's me. I don't got long, I got someone—"

"Tawana. You got Tawana connecting you. Get it right, now."

"Be easy, Tawana. You know how they are with these three-way calls, and I don't have much time before they end this. Cartier, look, I couldn't call your cell phone collect, so Tawana is doing me this solid. I got jammed up when I left you the other night. The cops caught me ridin' dirty. The only person who knew my movements was Ryan. He called for me to meet him—look, that's a long story, but if I get the chance, if you ever decide to come and see me—a nigga will be out of commission for a while—I'll kick it with you. But right now you're in danger. Niggas know I ain't there to hold you down, so you gotta bounce. And I mean, right now. Don't trust no—"

The line went dead.

Sleep-deprived Cartier hopped up, her mind racing. Yes, she was thankful beyond words that he wasn't dead, but the urgency in his voice spooked her. He was the second person in a short timeframe to tell her that she couldn't trust those around her.

"Ma!" Cartier screamed.

Within seconds, Trina came bursting into the kitchen. "It's time. We gotta go! That was just Head. He's alive, but he said that niggas are gonna be gunning for me and that I shouldn't trust no one."

"OK, I'm going to get the kids up."

"Don't take anything. Don't wash them up, nothing. I'm going to get the car and bring it around front. Wait until I call before you come downstairs."

Just as Cartier began pulling on her jeans, Christian came out of her room with wide eyes. Cartier tucked her pistol in her waistband and pulled on her T-shirt to conceal it. Before she could pull on her sneakers, Christian began whining.

"I wanna go."

"Quiet! And go and get dressed with your grandmother. We're all going. Mommy's going to get the car."

The defiant little girl wasn't having it. She truly missed her mother, who had been running the streets for weeks. "Please, Momma, I wanna go with you. I'll be good, I promise."

Cartier looked at her little face and couldn't resist. She hurried and began to dress Christian.

Trina came out of her room fully dressed. "Look, you taking too long, Cartier. Get the others dressed, and I'll go and get the car."

Fendi, Prada, and Jason Jr., ran down the stairs, while Cartier carried Christian, who was in baby mode. She had her head tucked snugly under Cartier's chin as her small hands gripped her mother tightly.

As Cartier approached the opening of the building, she could see Trina already out of the car and securing Jason Jr. in his car seat, while the others scrambled to put on their seatbelts.

The wild-eyed beauty did a slow trot up the block, like a racehorse about to compete, her gat draped conspicuously in her hands.

Instinctively Cartier dropped Christian and then caught her child with one arm just before she hit the ground. The frightened child shrilled in horror, as all of Cartier's attention went to protecting her child. The warm sensation plunged into Cartier's thigh, causing her to stumble forward.

As bullets whizzed by, Cartier kneeled down in an effort to use her body to shield her baby, but it was too late. She felt her child go limp and then drop down by her feet. The second bullet lodged into Cartier's abdomen, and the sensation was no longer warm. It felt as if someone had stuck firecrackers in her navel and lit them. She peered over and saw that Trina had taken her whole body and laid it across each child inside the car.

With blood oozing, and pain ripping through her whole body, Cartier finally mustered the strength to pull out her pistol and began bucking back. With a steady hand, she emptied her clip, but she wasn't sure she'd hit Marisol.

Just as Cartier was about to lose consciousness, she saw Marisol stand over her and then, *Boom!*

As Cartier closed her eyes, she felt a heavy body drop right next to her.

CHAPTER 31

Halo

The beeping from the ventilator roused Cartier awake. She was in minimal pain despite her injuries, thanks to the Demerol dripping through her IV. Three familiar faces sat around flipping through magazines and gossiping, while *E! True Hollywood Story* played on the television.

Trina noticed her stirring. "Cartier, you're awake."

Everyone rushed toward her side.

"I knew you wouldn't leave me." Trina could hardly believe her own reaction. She began sobbing uncontrollably as she reached down and gently embraced her daughter.

Janet stood behind Trina, rubbing her back for comfort. The ladies had been through so much spanning over four decades. Soon, Janet inched Trina out of the way and began planting wet kisses on Cartier's face, her tears dripping on Cartier's forehead.

The outpouring of emotion brought Cartier to tears. She realized she could have easily crossed over to the other side and left her family forever.

"It's a great day in the neighborhood," Janet joked to lighten the mood.

Finally she spoke through a hoarse, raspy voice. "How long have I been gone?"

"Three days," Trina answered. "The doctor said he wasn't sure you were going to pull through. You lost so much blood, they had to give you a transfusion."

The shootout with Marisol came rushing back. The look in her black eyes, the need for vengeance plastered on her face, the deep-seated hatred mirrored Cartier's feelings as well, but on that day, when Marisol got the drop on her, Cartier was frightened. She remembered that her knees buckled, her heart raced, and her hands trembled, all within a nanosecond.

"Oh, my God! Christian! Where's my baby?" Cartier screamed. Her heart monitor began to beep erratically. "Please—"

Both ladies hushed her. "Shhh!"

"She's fine," Trina said. "A bullet did graze her, but we just left her. She's in the children's ward. Fendi, Prada, and Jason Jr. are in there keeping her company."

"I need to see my baby. If anything had happened to her, I would have killed myself."

"Cartier, get yourself together. The kids have been through a lot. They don't need to see you agitated. It'll cause them more trauma. Gather your thoughts, and we'll have the nurse get the wheelchair and take you over there."

Cartier sat back and tried to steady her breathing. "Where's Marisol? Did she get hit too?"

"She dead," Trina said matter-of-factly. "It was only one bullet, but it did the deed. Li'l Momma got the drop on her, and at the right moment. You owe her your life, Cartier."

Cartier was relieved. She remembered letting off a few shots before she blacked out, but she didn't know if she'd actually hit anything. She looked Li'l Momma directly in her eyes and mouthed the words, "Thank you." Cartier was weighed down with unspeakable gratitude.

"You know you got an angel on your shoulders," Li'l Momma told her.

"Two," Cartier replied, referring to Shanine and Monya.

Her words made Janet smile.

"Li'l Momma, thank you. Words can't begin to say what my heart feels."

"Girl, please. You would have done the same shit for me. And, as you said, you do have angels holding you down because I wasn't even supposed to be on your block that early. I couldn't sleep the night before, and I decided to walk over to your house and see if you wanted to go to McDonald's and get breakfast. Like, what adult craves McDonald's?"

Everyone laughed.

Trina and Janet stayed for hours and took Cartier to see Christian. When they finally left, Cartier realized that Bam hadn't come.

"Where's Bam?" she asked Li'l Momma.

Li'l Momma waited for the nurse to finish checking Cartier's vital signs. When she left, Li'l Momma whispered, "She's taking a long nap."

"What? Who got at her? I took out Ryan, you took out Marisol, who else is out there?" Cartier was tired of exchanging bullets with rival crews.

"I gotta give it to you straight. I deaded Bam."

"You?"

"She was a double agent, Cartier. After you and Christian got rushed to the hospital, Trina confided in me and Janet about what Wonderful had told you. We all sat down going through Ryan's rolodex, just as you had begun, and listed under Maria's Daycare was Bam's telephone number. Trina wanted to handle Bam herself, but I told her I needed to do it. I had to look in Bam's eyes and try to understand how she could throw away decades of friendship. I don't know when she flipped, but she did. She didn't have a beef with me. It was you and Jason she wanted to see dead. She let them know that Jason was out of the hospital and meeting us at Trina's. That's how they got the drop on him. And she also told Marisol where to find you."

The news was unbearable. "Are you sure?"

"She told me herself."

"She told you?"

"After you came out of ICU, I cruised by to see her. There wasn't any way I was going in there blazing. What if Ryan's sneaky ass was setting up Bam? So I approached it giving her the benefit of the doubt, something I knew Trina wouldn't do. Not when her daughter and granddaughter were laid up in the hospital. Bam was high as a kite, puffing on that shit, talking all fast. She was bouncing off the walls. Check it, she started talking crazy about how you were like the Teflon don of Brooklyn, able to take ten bullets and still be breathing. Then she put on 50 Cent's "Many Men," and began singing the lyrics. I was already peeping that her tone didn't sound too happy that you were alive. Next thing I know, she started acting all paranoid. She kept peering out her window, toting her .45. When I asked who she was looking for, she said you.

"About an hour of trying to put together all her crazy statements, I pieced together that she thought that Big Mike would come into her dreams at night and tell her that she had to avenge his death." Li'l Momma shook her head. "I had to do it, Cartier. She forced my hand. There wasn't any way she could get a pass, going against the grain as she did. And I couldn't wait to see what you'd wanna do when you woke up. What if Big Mike came and told her ass to off me?" Li'l Momma laughed at the silliness of Bam's mind. "I always said she wasn't ever too right after Donnie beat her brains out."

"Damn! I just find it too hard to believe that Bam would go out like that. I mean we're sisters . . . all of us. And to think she would really want me dead is something I might not fully comprehend, Li'l Momma." Cartier began to choke up. To hear that Bam was gone was overwhelming. "If she couldn't handle the Big Mike shit she should have tried to kick my ass, you know, curse me out—spit in my face, but for her to go and plot with Ryan and Marisol shows me that she wasn't in her right mind. I told her to stop smoking that shit."

"If it's any consolation, that was the hardest thing I had to do."

"I know it was." Cartier looked off toward the window. Everyone had avoided the topic, but when she first came to from the medication, she purposely didn't ask because she didn't want to know. Finally, she asked. "Anyone heard from Jason? Did what Wonderful said have any truth to it?"

The silence nearly killed Cartier. When Li'l Momma's eyes went toward the floor, it confirmed what she already knew.

"You sure you wanna hear this?"

"Li'l Momma, he's my husband. I need to know what happened to him."

"They did torture him, Cartier. They did things to him that the medical examiner said was inhumane. He had over one hundred tiny knife pricks throughout his whole body, missing fingers and toes, his arms were broken in several places with such force, they figured a bat was used. He had burn marks all over his upper and lower body where someone either used a lighter and held it until his skin began to burn, or they used a blow torch. Just sick shit that no one believes really happens. His body was found in the one abandoned building on Miller Avenue by some neighborhood kids. He went unclaimed for days in the coroner's office as a John Doe because he didn't have any identification on him. Then Trina went to the precinct and filled out a missing person's report. They called her nine hours later to ID his body."

Cartier's chest tightened at the news. That meant when she went to kill Ryan, Jason was with her. And when Marisol rolled up, Jason was there too. Cartier realized she didn't have two angels but three.

Li'l Momma left Cartier to come to terms with the events, and promised to return.

EPILOGUE

New Beginnings

Despite Bam's betrayal, Cartier still paid for her funeral and gave her a grand homecoming. Cartier picked out an all-white lacquer casket and dressed her in an all-white Chanel dress. A white horse and carriage carried Bam's body through the neighborhood with her stepmother and family sitting stoically in the back. Bam looked like a sleeping angel. Cartier hoped in her heart that Bam would meet Shanine and Monya in heaven; that they'd still be crew on the other side. Cartier couldn't help but feel somewhat responsible for Bam's actions, but there wasn't anything she could do. The past was the past, and she had her future to think about. Bam was laid to rest on Tuesday, and then they laid Jason to rest on Wednesday.

The kids took it harder than she thought. Each night they would cry and ask for their daddy. Cartier requested a closed casket for fear that Cee Cee and Jason Jr. might have nightmares. She picked out a lavish platinum and chrome casket with a plaque that said H8TER, a gesture she was sure Jason would have appreciated. She knew she would miss him. Despite all they'd been through, he was still her husband and the father of her only child. And although she finally refused to listen to the audio tape of his murder, she believed Wonderful when he said Jason wouldn't give her up. Finally, she had affirmation that he truly loved her too.

❦

On her way to the house Cartier began to feel nostalgic. As she wheeled her car toward 555 Dolphin Court Lane, she rolled down her window so she could hear and smell the ocean. The air was crisp, moist, clean, as she inhaled the salty atmosphere. She took a look at the tree-lined block with expansive mansions and realized how beautiful the neighborhood was. Not just her house, but the overall look and feel of the whole area was breathtaking. Cartier felt she might have taken that for granted before. She'd come a long way from hugging the block and boosting to actually living out a dream that most people had, which was to escape poverty.

Now her future was unsteady. Jason was murdered, Head was in jail, and she had a family of six to provide for. Sure, she had investments, but she didn't have liquid. Putting the house on the market was her only choice, but how long would it take to sell?

"Ma, what time are the movers coming?"

"They're supposed to be there around nine this morning. They said it will take them all day to pack everything up, and it's going to cost you a grip. I don't know why we didn't just gather all our friends to help us pack ourselves."

"Because I didn't want to inconvenience anyone."

"Shit. They would have done it to us and not given it a second thought."

"Maybe." Cartier shrugged her shoulders. "But it's already done. The movers will pack up everything the correct way, and honestly, I don't have the strength to be wrapping plates and folding sweaters. That's the last thing I wanna do."

Trina didn't respond. She knew her daughter had a lot on her mind.

When they pulled up, there were two large 18-wheeler semi-tractor trailers. The eight-man crew had arrived early, ready to work.

The project manager, a brawny, broad-shouldered Russian with blond hair and piercing blue eyes, approached Cartier's driver's side door, clipboard in hand. "Mrs. Timmons-Payne?"

"Hi. How are you?" Cartier replied, extending her hand for a shake. "I see you got here early."

"Yeah, we should begin as soon as possible. This is"— He looked down at his clipboard—"being packed up to go back to our storage unit until further notice, correct?"

"Just until we can find a new place." Cartier felt a little embarrassed, which she couldn't understand. They'd been in the house less than a year and already needed to relocate. She was sure the neighbors, all white, would be elated.

Cartier showed everyone in and headed upstairs to her bedroom to gather all her important documents—

children's birth certificates, social security cards, bank statements, and credit cards. She toyed with the idea of bringing all her photo albums too, but quickly thought against it. She didn't need the extra baggage.

She had been inside her walk-in closet for almost two hours looking through her documents when Trina found her.

"Hey, what are you doing in here?" Trina asked.

"Just trying to weed out what's important. I would hate to need any paperwork and have to go fishing through a packed storage unit."

Trina looked at the large pile of photos. "You taking these?"

"Nah."

"Why not?"

"We'll get them soon as we find our new home."

"But what if something happens to them? I hear that storage units get looted all the time."

"Ma, that's the last thing someone will steal, family photos. And everything else will be insured."

Trina could sense a sadness in her oldest child. "Do you need help?"

"Yeah. Could you continue looking through all this paperwork for me and gather the important stuff? I have something I need to do."

Cartier walked to her sitting area in her room and sat down to write a letter.

What up, Head

Or should I say boo? I know you didn't ask for me to be there for you, to hold you down while you do your bid. I'm hoping that's because you know that I will. There isn't any way I'd let you do this bid without being at your side. Whatever they give you, five, ten, fifteen years, just know that we're going to do those years together.

I'm not Tawana, I'm Cartier, and she and I are cut from a different cloth. You walked into my life, and I felt love unconditionally. Don't ever question my heart. This isn't about Jason not being here. I chose you the first night we made love, and you said you chose me the first day you saw me. I believe that things happen for a reason.

I'm packing up my family and moving out of New York. I'm not sure where yet, but know that I won't ever miss ONE visit. And I'll always bless your commissary and you'll always receive a weekly letter or card. I know what it's like to lose the ones you love most while being locked down, and I want you to know that if you don't have anyone else, you have me. I hate to say this for the first time in a letter, but I love you, heart, mind, body and soul.

An honest woman
Cartier

Trina had called Cartier's name twice before her daughter actually heard her. Cartier was engrossed in re-reading her letter, hoping it said everything she wanted to say. Finally she relaxed. *It's all about actions.* Her actions would solidify her words.

"Cartier."

"Yes?"

"I think you need to see this. It might not be anything, but then again it could be everything." Trina rushed over with a plastic baggy containing paperwork from Chase bank.

"What's this?"

"It's a key to a safety deposit box, and you're listed as a second signer."

"What? How could that be? Wouldn't I have had to be with him to be a second signer?" Cartier peered at the signature line. Trina was right. She was listed as a second signer, but it wasn't her handwriting.

"Look, figure out all the particulars later. You need to go down to this bank with your identification and see what's up. For all we know, the person who posed as you could have already been there."

Cartier rushed out of the house and sped off to Chase. She approached the teller and asked to gain access to her safety deposit box.

"Sure. Have a seat, and our branch manager will be with you shortly."

Cartier walked over to the set of chairs, but she couldn't sit down. Her palms were sweating, and her heart was racing.

"Ma'am."

"Yes?" Cartier turned to face a well-groomed, conservative-looking gentleman clad in a three-piece suit and tie.

"Could you follow me?"

The manager led Cartier downstairs to the lower level, where the boxes were located. He stood behind the desk and pulled out the registry. "What's your box number?"

"Umm, three, zero, eight, one." Cartier swallowed hard.

After flipping briefly through an index box, he pulled out a card. "Do you have identification?"

Cartier tossed him her license.

He looked at it. "Could you sign here for signature verification?"

"Sure." Quickly Cartier tried to recall the signature on the paperwork. *Why didn't I practice before running into the bank?* She tried her best to replicate the signature, remembering that the *C* was pronounced and the rest of her name illegible.

The bank manager hardly glanced at the signature before walking her through a large vault with over one thousand boxes. They both stood in front of box 3081. He took out his master key and opened his side before telling Cartier to open hers.

Fumbling with her key, Cartier wondered if he could see her hands trembling. Once it was opened, she stood back and watched him pull a somewhat large, heavy box and place it into a private room.

"I'll be outside," he said. "Take your time."

As soon as he closed the door, Cartier opened her future. There was all the money Jason had taken from the house. Over a million dollars in crisp bills neatly stacked in an 18 x 20 box. Tears of relief trickled down Cartier's cheeks. She now had a chance. A new beginning. Money to take care of herself and her family.

She thought of Jason. He would have wanted it this way. Christian and Jason Jr. would benefit from his life in the streets. She'd make sure to always tell them about their father and how much he loved them.

As Cartier looked at the box she realized Jason had thought of everything. Inside, tucked on the side of the stainless steel box, was a black duffle bag. She grinned. And she kept grinning as she waltzed out of the bank after making a hefty withdrawal.

"Hey, Li'l Momma."

"What's up, girl?"

"Life is good."

Li'l Momma was so glad to hear such a positive response from Cartier after all she'd been through. "I'm glad you're feeling better. I just want you to know that, whatever you need, I'm still here for you. Babysitter, sister, friend, punching bag"—Li'l Momma laughed—"I got you."

"I know you do. Listen," Cartier said, barely able to contain her excitement, "I found the money Jason had stolen from our family."

"Get the fuck out!" Li'l Momma exclaimed, a rush of excitement traveling through her body. "God is good."

"Most definitely. He's good to you too because I got two hundred large with your name written all over it."

It was at that moment that Li'l Momma understood the meaning of Cartel.

"I don't know what to say."

"You don't have to say anything. I'll drop it off before I hit the road."

"Have you decided on where you're going?"

"Not yet, but I won't be too far from you or my man."

"Head?"

"Yeah. He said he's going to make an honest woman out of me."

"You're still going to marry him?"

"First chance I get."

MIAMI, MEET BROOKLYN

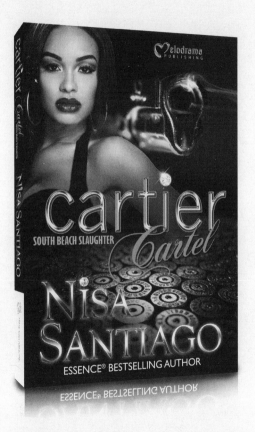

Keep Reading for a Sneak Peek!

EXCERPT FROM CARTIER CARTEL PART 3: SOUTH BEACH SLAUGHTER

Chapter One

Miami, Florida, with its sandy beaches, year-round warm weather, and alluring club life was a direct contrast to the cold, changeable weather of Philadelphia. Cartier had nothing against Philly, but Miami was a better town for her. Not only was she tired of the cold and snow, but Philly was also too close to New York. Wanting the best for her family, she needed to be somewhere far from New York and away from the turbulent lifestyle she'd once lived. That meant staying out of the game and keeping a low profile. The violence and the killings had taken a toll on her and her family, so she wanted to put as much distance as possible between herself and her beloved Brooklyn.

She'd only lasted a few months in Philly, until one day she came upon Shorty Dip, a familiar face from Brooklyn who recognized her. There was no telling who was still holding grudges. That spooked her. Cartier had made a lot of enemies up North, and to constantly have to look over her shoulder wasn't something she wanted for her family. Especially with young kids to care for. After Jason got himself murdered and Cartier got herself and Christian shot up, Cartier had never felt so vulnerable. Losing Monya, Shanine, Bam and finally Jason made her will to live that much stronger.

Cartier packed up her things and, along with her mother, Trina, her daughter, Christian, and her sisters Fendi and Prada, headed down I-95 until there wasn't any more highway left to travel. Janet, Trina's best friend and Monya's mother, said she couldn't bear to be so far away from her grandson, Jason Jr., so, reluctantly, Cartier agreed to have her step son in Miami six weeks out of each summer.

It was only a matter of weeks before Cartier and Trina clashed. You see, Miami is a party town and the weather is always hot and tropical. The problem was that there were two mothers: Cartier and Trina—and neither one wanted to parent.

"Now you done gone out every night this week, Cartier. Ain't nobody your live-in nanny!" Trina barked. She was heated because she wanted to hit the clubs so she could meet some of these Puerto Rican or Cuban men that were floating around the city. Trina was more than ready to get her fuck on. "You got a daughter to look after."

"And you don't? Last I checked, Fendi and Prada call you 'Mommy'!"

"Cartier, you better watch your mouth . . ."

"Look who's talking!"

"That's right, I'm talking!" Trina exploded. "I take care of mines!"

Cartier rolled her eyes. "No, I take care of you and yours, and mines! So if I want to go out every now and then to shake my ass, you should be a little more understanding."

"What the fuck you just said, bitch?"

"Which part didn't you hear?"

Cartier was being belligerent, which drove Trina bananas. "Keep it up, Cartier, and I'ma put my foot in ya ass!"

"You in here screaming and acting all dumb 'cuz I wanna go out? Why you hatin'?" Cartier took one last look in the mirror at her silhouette. "You too old to be hitting the club anyways. Ain't no niggas gonna be checking for you."

Trina's feelings were a little hurt. When she looked in the mirror, she saw a good-looking female staring back at her. She didn't think she looked like a fortysomething grandmother and mother of three. The word old stung. She marched into her bedroom, overlooking the Atlantic Ocean, and called her best friend.

Cartier could hear her mother get on the phone with Janet. Trina began to tell her how she was moving back to Brooklyn and how ungrateful Cartier was after all she'd done for her.

"That li'l ugly bitch think she cute," Trina could be heard saying. "I'ma leave her bad-luck ass right in this city! She think these new Puerto Rican muthafuckers like her stink-ass Brooklyn attitude? She gonna get a rude awakening!"

The gleaming black Range Rover made its way across the MacArthur Causeway, headed toward South Beach. The eighty-five-thousand-dollar truck was a gift to herself. Cartier always moved around in style, and she had enough cash to splurge on herself and her family. She was living large off the money she'd found in the safe-deposit box that belonged to her dead husband, Jason. It was enough money to keep her afloat and to continue living the diva lifestyle for a long while. She had her peoples staying in a high-rise condo on Brickell Avenue, a thirty-five-story building that offered an unobstructed view of the ever-changing Miami skyline.

Cartier was proud of her accomplishments. She was one of a select few to leave the game alive and still live a life of luxury with her family. She had paid her dues in the streets, doing her dirt, busting her gun, surviving an assassination attempt, and even serving seven years in prison. Now it was time to live happily ever after. But Cartier knew life wasn't a fairy tale, and even though Miami was miles away from Brooklyn, she had sense enough to know that danger was everywhere, so she kept her gun close at all times.

She felt like a queen in her black chariot with "Started From the Bottom" by Drake blasting in the truck. The weather was warm and balmy, and she was ready to show off the shape she got from her momma. Clad in a form-fitting dress that hugged her luscious curves, her red-bottoms pressed against the accelerator, taking the Range Rover to 75 mph.

The sun had set long ago, creating a temperate evening over the city of Miami, which had lit up in a colorful hue that could be seen from miles away. The closer Cartier drove toward South Beach, the thicker the traffic became. South Beach was a major destination for both American and international tourists, with hundreds of nightclubs, restaurants, boutiques, and hotels.

A brown-skinned cutie in her late twenties, Cartier knew she could never get tired of the club scene. She'd done the wife thing—which didn't work out. She'd tried the "hold your man down while he's locked down" thing—which didn't work out. Now, she was doing her—which seemed to be working out great. She looked good and felt terrific. Cartier knew that Trina was getting fed up, but it wasn't anything a shopping spree and some quality family time couldn't fix.

She came to a stop in front of Buck 15, a small underground bar and lounge with artistic furnishing and a loft feel. Her pricey Range Rover blended in smoothly with the Rolls-Royce Phantom, cocaine-colored Bentley, S550 Benz, Corvettes, Porsches, and Audi Q7s parked on the busy street. She stepped out of her truck feeling like a celebrity. The second her pricey red-bottoms touched the pavement, all eyes were on her. She strutted toward the front entrance with a smirk. She was so Brooklyn.

Cartier was cool with one of the security guards and eased inside. She was extra happy tonight. She was excited about her good friend, Li'l Mama, flying in tomorrow evening from New York into Miami International. It had been a long while since the two founding members from the Cartier Cartel had seen each other, so they had a lot of catching up to do.

Buck 15 was blaring with Flo Rida, and the patrons were jumping up and down, bouncing around the place, looking electrified. Cartier's eyes scanned the club, searching for Quinn, who had to be nowhere else but in the VIP section, where she lived and breathed, popping bottles with her peoples. Cartier strutted toward the VIP area, moving through the thick crowd. Bitches were hating—giving hard stares—and niggas were craving to push up. Cartier had edge that didn't go unnoticed. It was a mix of sex appeal and grit. As the strobe lights bounced off her, the crowd parted to allow her through.

She spotted her girl Quinn seated in the VIP, surrounded by the Ghost Ridas, her brother's Miami gang. Since Cartier's arrival in Miami, Quinn had become a really good friend to her. The two had met in Club 01 a few months earlier. That night Quinn had complimented Cartier on her shoes, and they started talking, and had become inseparable.

Quinn, Mexican-born and Miami-raised, was a female with a body to die for. She had raven-black hair, tanned skin, and dark, hypnotic eyes that could cut through a brick wall. At five eight, she was definitely eye candy in the club in her deep purple low-cut dress with the ultra-plunging neckline. Her strong, defined legs stretched out in a pair of Fendi pumps.

Quinn had a strong predilection for the brothers. In fact, she loved to have a big, black dick inside of her. There was something about the brothers that made her weak, which sometimes caused unrest with her blood brother and his gang. But Quinn didn't give a fuck. She had earned their respect, because she was a bad bitch who was down for whatever. She downed her umpteenth drink, laughing with the Ghost Ridas, over a dozen deep and sporting their gang colors, purple and black.

As Cartier stepped inside the area, Quinn shouted out, "Is that my fuckin' bitch right there?" She stood up to greet Cartier with a hug and kisses to both cheeks.

"Hey, Quinn," Cartier greeted with a smile.

"Have a seat, bitch," Quinn said jokingly. "What you drinking?"

Having grown up around killers all her life, Cartier took her seat among the wolves. Any friend of Quinn's was a friend of hers.

Quinn removed the Moët bottle from its icy chill and poured Cartier a glass, while the tattooed gangsters of the Ghost Ridas, clad in leather vests, purple Ts, jeans and heavy jewelry were laughing it up and drinking heavily.

Cartier leaned back against the soft-cushioned banquette that ran along the VIP room and crossed her legs. Her eyes scanned the room, looking for any dude with potential. There was so much money inside the club;

so many niggas who were boss of their empires, just as Cartier was boss of hers. She took a sip of Moët, as the club came alive to Rihanna's "Diamonds."

"So, your friend from New York is comin' tomorrow, right?" Quinn asked.

Cartier nodded. "Yup."

"You need me to roll wit' you?"

"If you want."

"Bitch, you know I'm down."

Cartier was happy to hear that. She was hoping that the two didn't bump heads and would get along with each other, knowing that Li'l Mama could be rough around the edges and that Quinn was a hardcore bitch. The last thing she needed was some beef between her longtime friend and her newfound friend.

"Hey, Quinn, who's the chola?" one of the Ghost Ridas asked, eyeing Cartier like she was his property. "She down to get wit' the homies?"

Cartier looked up at the man unperturbed.

Quinn erupted with, "Yo, Tumble, chill ay, you my vato, but don't play my homegirl. You drunk, yo. Fall back." She stood up to make her point clear.

Tumble stood over six feet tall, and he was muscular, with two dark teardrops under his right eye. He was clutching a bottle of Henny Black in his hand. It was evident he was a little tipsy.

Tumble glanced at Cartier. "Chido. No disrespect, Quinn." He took a few steps back. "Maybe another time."

Cartier already knew his type. He was a killer. It

showed in his eyes, and was literally written on his face. Though Quinn had the leash around him tight, Cartier knew he was the type of dude that didn't ask for permission to get what he wanted.

"Don't mind him, Cartier," Quinn said, moving her hands around wildly. "He a fool. Nigga knows better than to disrespect any of my peoples."

"I'm cool, Quinn." Cartier shrugged her shoulders, dismissively. "It ain't even that serious."

"I feel you, mama." A now more relaxed Quinn took a swig from the Moët bottle.

Cartier was on her third drink and feeling nice. When she felt her iPhone vibrate and ring in her clutch, she quickly reached into it to answer the call. There was no number on her caller ID, but she answered anyway, plugging one finger into her left ear and leaning over with the phone against her right.

"Hello," she said, trying to hear over the earsplitting music. "Hello," she repeated, but there was nothing but silence on the other end. She looked down to see the screen pop up on her phone. The caller had hung up.

Cartier tossed her phone back into her clutch, looking somewhat worried. It was the third such phone call she'd received this evening.

"You okay?" Quinn asked.

She nodded.

Cartier sat for a moment, her high spirits changing somewhat. She began to think about her family.

She tapped Quinn on her shoulder. "I gotta make a

phone call. I'll be in the bathroom."

"You sure everything's okay?" Quinn repeated with concern.

"Yeah. I just gotta call home."

Cartier stood up and hurried from the VIP area and walked toward the ladies' bathroom. She pushed the door open and went into her clutch again and pulled out her cell phone. She leaned against the sink and dialed home.

The phone rang three times then Trina picked up. "What, Cartier?"

"Ma, everything okay?"

"Yeah, everything's okay. Why you asking?"

"I dunno. Where's Christian?"

"I just put her ass to bed. She's fast asleep. What's wrong?"

"Nothing . . ."

"You sure?"

"Yeah."

"Ya ass feeling guilty, right? 'Cuz you keep leaving me in here to babysit these kids."

"Nah, it ain't even like that. I just had a strange feeling."

"Don't worry about us, Cartier," Trina said coolly. "This ain't New York. Nobody knows us down here. Everything's fine. Go and have a good time. I'm here watchin' a movie and the house is quiet."

"Okay, Ma. Thanks. I'll see you later."

Cartier hung up, feeling somewhat relieved, but that

strange feeling still swirled around in her stomach. She turned to look at her image in the large mirror, sighing heavily. She was alone in the bathroom and could hear the muffled music from the club. She checked herself quickly and applied more lip gloss to her full lips. "I need some fuckin' dick. I'm turning into an uptight, paranoid bitch," she chuckled to herself as she walked out.

As the party continued, Cartier had a nice chat with Ranger, a well-respected O.G. in Ghost Ridas. In his mid-thirties, he was Miami-born with Mexican and Dominican blood. Swathed with gang tattoos and nice jewelry, he stood six-four.

Cartier was enjoying their talk, but then she noticed she was being watched by a dark stranger from across the bar. His gaze was intense. When she returned his stare, he never broke eye contact. At first she expected his eyes to soften; perhaps he would walk over and push up or, as a flirty gesture, send her a bottle of champagne. So it came, at first, as a blow to her ego. And then the hair on the back of her neck began to stand up. If he wanted her to be intimidated, she wasn't going to show it. He glared and she glared back.

Ranger noticed she was distracted, and then he noticed the distraction. "You know dude?"

Cartier shook her head.

Ranger took off with Cartier on his heels. She was drunk and was ready to set it off. Club or no club, she wanted it to go down.

The dark stranger, who was nursing a beer at the

edge of the bar, didn't flinch. As the couple approached he stood his ground.

"Yo, homes, you got a problem wit' my lady?"

The man slowly turned to see that he was surrounded by Ranger, Cartier, and now a few Ghost Ridas. He removed himself from the barstool but kept a cool demeanor. "No," he said. "No problem with her at all. My bad if I offended anyone."

"Leave, muthafucka, before I let loose some of my goons and you won't leave at all."

The man smirked and held up his hands in surrender. "Not a problem."

Cartier wasn't going to allow it to end so easily. She picked up a random drink and tossed it into his face.

"Do we have a problem now?"

The man wiped the dripping liquid off his dark-chocolate skin and gritted his teeth.

"Nah, we still don't have a problem."

Had this been a New York nightclub, he would have had his guts stomped out. Cartier was wondering what she had to do for the Ghost Ridas to teach this lame-ass dude a lesson. She could see something in his eyes that she didn't like. Had the Cartel been at her side, he would have been shot or stabbed the fuck up by now. From her peripheral vision she could see security trying to make their way through the crowd.

Amped up on liquid courage, Cartier wanted to fan the fire. She lunged toward him but was held back by Ranger. He grabbed both her wrists as she tried to swing, wildly. Cartier looked, and Quinn wasn't anywhere to be found, which left a salty taste in her mouth. There was an unspoken code between girlfriends—have my back at all times!

"Ay, yo! Chill, mama!" Ranger said, as he struggled with the feisty female.

Cartier watched as the stranger backpedaled toward the door before he made his exit. He glanced at Cartier one last time, took his index finger and made a sweeping slit your throat gesture, sending a creepy chill down her spine. He had New York written all over him. She knew he could be trouble.

"Did you see what he just did?!" she screamed. "He said he's gonna kill me!"

The Ghost Ridas looked at the young troublemaker and shrugged off her theatrics. She wasn't one of them.

They came out tonight to have a good time and at the moment she was blowing everyone's high. They flexed their presence and authority and was shown respect without busting their guns or creating chaos. Truth be told, neither one of them was ready to make the papers defending a black chick from up North.

Cartier was furious. She sulked around the club until she found Quinn, hemmed up against a wall with some dude whispering in her ear.

Cartier roared, "Where the fuck you been?"

Quinn was taken aback. Surely Cartier wasn't talking to her. "Huh?"

"Yo, I'm out."

Quinn blinked a couple times. "Why you leavin', chica? You just got here."

Cartier rolled her eyes and pushed her way through the crowd. Originally, she was going to ask Quinn to gather up a few Ridas and walk her to her car. But at the moment, she was so heated and filled with so much anger and rage that she didn't want any backup. She was in I wish a nigga would mode.

Cartier exited the club and rushed home to check on her family. She entered the condo and found her mother sleeping on the couch and Fendi, Prada, and Christian asleep in their bedrooms.

She was somewhat relieved, but she couldn't get over the creep from the club. What was that all about? And why wasn't Quinn around to have her back? Did she not notice all the commotion in the club? For Quinn to have all of a sudden disappeared didn't sit too well with Cartier.

As Cartier peeled off her clothes and hopped into a much-needed hot shower, the only silver lining was that her one true friend, Li'l Mama, would be arriving, tomorrow. She couldn't wait for their reunion.

FANCY'S BACK
AND SHE'S ON THE RISE

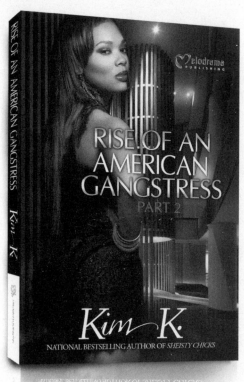

RISE OF AN AMERICAN GANGSTRESS

Melodrama
PUBLISHING

RISE OF AN
AMERICAN
GANGSTRESS
PART 2

Kim K.

Kim K.

NATIONAL BESTSELLING AUTHOR OF *SHEISTY CHICKS*

THE STREETS AREN'T
READY FOR THIS BAD GIRL

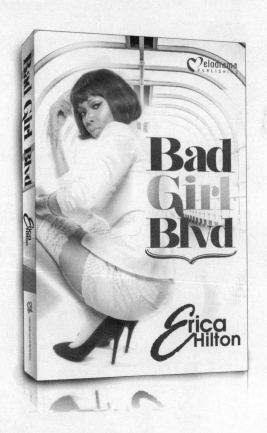